Sustainable Economic Development and Environment

India and Other Low Income Economies (LIEs)

Edited by

Raj Kumar Sen

Kartik C. Roy

ATLANTIC

PUBLISHERS & DISTRIBUTORS (P) LTD

in collaboration with

International Institute for Development Studies (IIDS)

Published by

ATLANTIC

PUBLISHERS & DISTRIBUTORS (P) LTD

7/22, Ansari Road, Darya Ganj, New Delhi-110002
Phones : +91-11-40775252, 40775214, 23273880, 23275880
Fax: +91-11-23285873
Web: www.atlanticbooks.com
E-mail: orders@atlanticbooks.com

Branch Office: Chennai
Phones : +91-44-48531784, 28291383
E-mail: chennai@atlanticbooks.com

Printed & bound in India by Atlantic Print Services

Preface

The decade of the 1990s has been designated as the International Decade of Sustainable Development by the United Nations. In fact no single issue in recent times has grasped the attention of thinking people worldwide so completely as the problem of sustainability. Yet the concept itself is illusive and it means many things to many people. Different disciplinary paradigms portray sustainability differently.

The International Institute for Development Studies naturally paid attention to this sustainability debate in its very First bi-annual International Conference (Calcutta) on Development and Future Studies, where one of the four panels of discussions was selected as Sustainability of Development: Economic, Sociological and Environmental Aspects. In reality, economic, sociological and environmental aspects—all have a bearing on whether sustainable development can be achieved. The present Volume—Sustainable Economic Development and Environment: India and Other Low Income Economies (LIEs) has included as many as seven articles which were presented/contributed to this conference. The IIDS Second International Conference (Perth) also deliberated on the theme albeit indirectly in its technical session on: Growth, Environment, Ecology and Ethics. Five articles included in this Volume are outcome of this conference.

The fourteen articles selected in this edited Volume address to a wide range of issues and aspects related to the sustainability of development though most of them concentrated on socio-economic and environmental implications of economic development in the context of low income economies in general and India in particular. Of course large units like country groups (*e.g.* SAARC) and smaller ones like village, island etc. also figured and authors also studied issues like the sustainability of agriculture and importance of the eco-system. The role of institutions and information system in the perspective of global sustainability are other important issues deliberated in this volume.

The first four articles (*Roy* and *Sen; Chakraborty; Sen; Devasthali*) of this volume discussed in general the major issues of sustainability of development for the LIEs and the socio-economic perspective of this concept including the alternative development paradigms. The economic agenda for the 1990s and beyond also formed part of the discussion. Economics of environment was then discussed in the context of sustainability as the major theme in a number of subsequent articles. It is analysed for the developing countries in general (*Manonmoney*), for the SAARC countries (*Guru*), for a state (*Yumnam*) (in the form of common property rights) and also for a village (*Rao*). The problem of environmental implication of economic development is also discussed in an input-output framework (*Prakash and Chowdhury*), in the context of population growth (*Konar*) and industrialisation in India (*Sablok*). The dwindling forests posing a threat to the environment of India and the problems and prospects for the sustainable growth of an island economy are dwelt upon in the next couple of articles (*Nath; Ghosh*). The volume ends with discussion of the role of information systems for sustainable development (*Harrison and Sharma*).

On behalf of the IIDS the editors sincerely hope that this volume will be in tune with the new found emphasis of economists and the wider community on the concept of sustainability. It may also prove useful to researchers and interesting to the general readers.

The IIDS likes to place on record its thanks to Dr. K.R. Gupta of Atlantic Publishers and Distributors, New Delhi for publishing this book in a most meticulous manner. It also thanks all others who have helped in the publication process in one way or another.

RAJ KUMAR SEN
KARTIK C. ROY

Contents

1

Major Issues in Sustaining Growth and Development in LDCs

Kartik C. Roy and Raj Kumar Sen

In sustaining growth and development in less developed countries, some major issues are identified in this article. These include health and education, appropriate technology, proper emphasis on agriculture and industry, adequate provision of infrastructure like power, transport, communication and effective administration, external resource flows and public debt etc. Higher returns on investment in education in terms of human capital formation and benefits of better health on workers' productivity are already well documented. Careful choice of technology is extremely important to form a sustainable basis for choosing amongst conflicting investment options. This is also true for striking an optimum balance for emphasis on agriculture and industry in adoption of appropriate economic policies. The crucial importance of adequate provision of infrastructure in sectors like power, transport and communication in the implementation and maintenance of projects are also highlighted. At the same time attention is drawn to the necessity of an efficient administration for their sustained growth. Similarly efficiency in the use of external resource flows in the form of foreign debt and investment determines the success of development process and also its sustainability.

Of course, in spite of favourable influences of all these factors identified, population growth at an unsustainable rate leading to excessive use of scarce resources can greatly undermine the capacity of the economy to sustain growth and development beyond the present and immediate future. All these call for effective co-operation between people, government, political parties and NGOs to achieve desired results.

Introduction

Since the dawn of civilization, human societies have been striving for the realisation of four cardinal values for mankind: (*i*) survival of the species, (*ii*) security in the life span of individual, (*iii*) material prosperity for ensuring survival and security and for continued expansion of the scope of wholesome living, and (*iv*) mental progress for unfolding the potential of each and every individual. However, the attainment of material prosperity and mental progress of human beings require, in the first instance, the provision of minimum food, shelter, clothing, housing, health care, education and transport. Fulfilment of these basic human needs will ensure the survival of the species and provide security in the life span of individual without which the attainment of material prosperity and mental progress will remain an elusive goal.

Health and Education

In 1890, 'Alfred' Marshall wrote that "health and strength, physical, mental and moral, are the basis of industrial wealth; while conversely the chief importance of material wealth lies in the fact that when wisely used, it increases the health and strength,—physical, mental and moral,—of the human race". Better diets, housing and control of communicable diseases raise the quality of life everywhere. By reducing illness, these improvements increase people's alertness, capacity for learning, and ability to cope with and enjoy life. By prolonging life, investments in knowledge and skill can be made even more worthwhile. The benefits of good health flow well into the future as a mother's good health strongly influences the early physical and mental development of her children. Better health apart from being a desirable end in itself also can release resources to be used to achieve other development goals. Better health and nutrition can raise worker's productivity, decrease the number of days they can become ill and can prolong their potential working lives. Health and nutrition also have long-run effects on productivity and output because they influence a child's ability and motivation to learn. Disease and malnutrition in infancy may retard mental development and illness and temporary hunger may reduce children's ability to concentrate and keep them away from school.

A number of studies have documented high returns on investment in education. World Bank research in returns on investment in education suggests that increasing the average amount of education of the labour force by one year, can raise GDP by 9 per cent per year for the first three years. Therefore, three years of education as compared with one can raise GDP by 27 per cent. By improving people's ability to acquire and use information, education deepens their understanding of themselves and the world and enriches their minds by broadening their experiences and improves the choices they make as consumers, producers and citizens. In developing countries the rate of expansion of education of female members has lagged behind that of male members. However, it is well recognised now that educated female members can make significant contribution to a country's development. Better educated women who are more informed about the value of health care and personal hygiene, tend to be less affected by the absence of community health programmes and tend to use them more frequently when they are available. Research also indicates the presence of negative correlation between females' education and infant mortality and fertility rates.

Appropriate Technology

Apart from health and education of population, the choice of technology is also a very important factor in development. The choice of technology is however greatly influenced by the relative factor prices in the country which in turn is influenced by the type of macroeconomic, and trade policies followed. Thus if, in a labour surplus country, the scarcity price of capital is lower than that of labour, capital intensive technology would tend to be used in development; but the relative factor pricing is also influenced by a domestic market sheltered from foreign competition by tariffs and other quantitative restrictions. Careful choice of technology is imperative to form a rational basis for choosing amongst conflicting investment options. Power intensive industrialisation and agricultural development can aggravate rather than mitigate the problems of poverty and unemployment. In the past, capital and labour were the only two factors needed to be considered in determining the choice of technology but in recent years such other factors as energy renewable and non-renewable and materials, natural and others, utilised per person employed per unit of output also have assumed considerable importance. Also it is important to take into account the external impact of a project on the environment as well as on the poor.

The Relative Emphasis on Agriculture and Industry

While the share of agriculture in the national income is expected to decline gradually over the longer terms, an attempt to force its decline faster can depress economic growth. A healthy agricultural sector can promote overall growth and influence the course of economic development by facilitating short-term adjustments. Hence, the application of appropriate economic policies and promotion of agriculture by making substantial investments in rural infrastructure are vital to the overall growth of these economies. The bias against agriculture is present in both economy-wide and sectoral policies pursued in many LDCs. This bias appears to have been intensified by the way developing countries have responded to changing economic circumstances. Since the 1960s, the general pattern of protection in developing countries has overwhelmingly favoured non-farm activities. Protection of import substitutes tends to raise the prices of protected goods relative to those of non-traded goods and thereby to encourage a shift in demand towards non-traded goods and the higher demand would generally cause prices to rise. As a result, the traded goods *i.e.* agricultural exports suffer because of the rise in cost to farmers of industrial inputs whose prices are determined by the prevailing international prices and of the appreciation of real exchange rate. Import-competing agricultural products, then suffer because prices of imported goods are kept at low levels to help urban consumers. This bias against agriculture caused by trade policy has been further strengthened by expansionary monetary and fiscal policies and an overvalued exchange rate regime in many LDCs. In countries with limited access to foreign capital and limited domestic savings, public sector deficits are financed mainly by printing more money. In other countries, capital in flows from abroad or increase in world prices of major exports lead to the appreciation of the real exchange rate and the application of expansionary fiscal policies. As a result, the rate of inflation in the domestic economy tends to be higher than in overseas countries; under such circumstances, those countries should try to adjust nominal exchange rate by the difference between domestic and international inflation. Instead, policies are directed to managing balance of payments by *ad hoc* trade and exchange controls. The nominal overvaluation of the currency which follows from these actions lowers the returns to agricultural exports and makes imports of food items cheaper relative to domestic substitutes.

Public expenditures in such infrastructure as irrigation, transport and communication, electricity, health services, education, research and extension are crucial to the performance of the agricultural sector. Countries which follow balanced pricing policies, through more competitive exchange rates and lower direct taxation of agriculture, also divert considerable public expenditure to the rural sector. This improves the performances of the agricultural sector which lifts the growth of industrial sector and overall growth rate of the economy.

Infrastructure—Power, Transport, Communication and Administration

Adequate provision of infrastructure is necessary for ensuring the successful implementation of all development projects as well as for maintaining those projects. Provision of infrastructure is also necessary to ensure the maintenance of infrastructure already created. Delays in the implementation of projects by two years due to inadequate planning and inadequate provision of infrastructure are known to have raised project implementation costs by as much as twenty per cent of the original estimate of costs. For making correct economic decisions at the planning and implementation stages of projects, operations research technique is being increasingly used in developing countries. For dissemination of benefits flowing from implementation of projects, efficient network of transport and communication are essential. Apart from helping to reduce costs, and to disseminate information, investments in infrastructure integrate markets. As a result, they make entrepreneur more productive. Infrastructure is, at least partly, a public good, as it is not easily divisible, it is difficult to exclude non-payers and is often subject to economies of scale, resulting in natural monopolies. Therefore, since private sector is unlikely to produce enough, the public production and provision of infrastructure services are vital for development. The productivity of projects in agriculture and industry also increases significantly as the share of overall public investments in GDP grows. However, carefully regulated private monopolies can also become efficient providers of infrastructure as evidenced from private bus operators in Ghana and in Calcutta, India; private contractors for water supply and refuse collection in Togo; private participation in power sector in Thailand and from private sector involvement in telecommunication in Chile, (erstwhile) Czechoslovakia, Hungary and Turkey. However, a weak and corrupt administration and inefficient management both at macroeconomic and enterprise levels can nullify much of the benefits to be derived from development projects. Governments are prone to fail, at least in economic terms, for various reasons. Since economic goals are not always their highest priorities, a combination of political objectives and constraints and weak administration may lead the governments to intervene in ways that are economically harmful. Also the consequences of economic intervention are difficult to predict and such intervention creates vested interests which make it difficult to change the policy. Excessive intervention breeds corruption which weakens a government's ability to carry out its functions efficiently. Bribery, nepotism and venality can cripple administration and dilute equity in the provision of government services and thereby also undermine social cohesiveness.

External Resource Flows and Public Debt

External resource flows can both be effective and ineffective in promoting and sustaining development. Sometimes aid can permit countries to postpone improving macroeconomic management and mobilizing domestic resources. Ready availability of foreign assistance to a country largely for political reasons can enable it to postpone political reform as happened in Pakistan. Foreign aid can also strengthen lobbies that have a strong vested interest in a distorted policy framework and thereby can make policy reform more difficult. Moreover, official aid can replace direct foreign investment, domestic savings, trade and other domestic commercial capital flows as the major source of investment and technology transfer. Large scale transfer of wheat and other food items is known to have depressed agricultural prices, postponed critical investments in rural infrastructure and ignore the need to build agricultural institutions. The widespread practice of tying aid to the purchase of equipment, shipping and technical advice from donor sources, have led funding agencies to transfer incompatible technologies and deliver conflicting projects and advice. On the other hand, external resources, if used effectively can improve the credibility of economic reform by providing assistance in designing reform packages and in holding down costs. External resources can help a country undertake investment and financial projects which otherwise could not have been undertaken and provide it with assistance in expanding much needed infrastructure. External aid can better social and economic policies. External aid agencies are becoming more and more sensitive to a project's effects on environment and social conditions. In most developing countries external capital is channeled largely through the government. The public sector also borrows heavily from domestic sources. Hence, the efficiency in the use of total debt rather than the size of the debt will determine the success of development programmes and the sustainability of development.

Population Growth, Natural Resources and Common Property Resources

However, even if the favourable influence of all these factors discussed above are present in the economy, development activities may still fail to improve the social and economic profile of the country, if population continues to grow at an unsustainable rate. Unchecked population growth leads to excessive use of scarce resources which undermines the capacity of the economy to sustain growth and development beyond the present and immediate future. The effects of population growth on natural resources, common property resources (CPR) and on the overall environment and their implications for sustainability of rural communities are well documented for many countries. The "green revolution" technology adopted in agriculture in India and in other countries primarily to achieve self-sufficiency in food production and supply has adversely affected the rural ecology and environments, and has reduced the supply to the poor of non-market goods from private property resources (PPR) and CPRs. The capacity of forests to provide food and other means of livelihood to the poor has been declining due, among other things, to increasing use of forest resources by larger number of people, commeicial exploitation of forests and to deforestation, climatic changes and fertility losses. In India, between 100 million and 150 million hectares of land are rapidly turning barren and one million hectares of crop land and grazing land are badly affected. On an average, every hectare loses twenty tonnes of top soil a year. Four million hectares have been swallowed up by ravines. In the famous Chambal Valley, more than 10 per cent of the villages are completely depopulated. Nearly seventy per cent of all available water in India is polluted. In many places the ground water table, has been going down thereby leaving the poor person's dugwell high and dry. Between a quarter to one half of the land brought under irrigation can go out of cultivation permanently because of soil salinity and water logging. The flood prone area has doubled over the last 10 years from 20 million to 40 million hectares. As a result, millions of people have been displaced and uprooted. The worst affected group in the ecologically devastated areas are undoubtedly landless and land poor women and children who have already been leading strenuous lives and have almost reached the limit of their carrying capacities.

Concluding Remarks

Such factors as discussed above interact with one another to produce an overall impact on all development programmes. Achieving a high rate of growth is not a desirable end in itself. Countries in South-East and North Asia have achieved high growth rates and have achieved considerable social progress. Nevertheless in these countries, there are millions who have hardly received any benefit from high growth. What is more important, however, is the capacity of developing countries to create and maintain conditions under which growth and development would be sustained so that large sections of their population who have been effectively left out of the benefits of development can enjoy some fruits of development. The task, therefore, facing developing economies is daunting no doubt but, change in government policy and attitude and effective co-operation between government, people, political parties, and non-government organisations can achieve desirable results.

REFERENCES

Chibber, A. and Wilton, J. (1986); Macro Economic Policies and Agricultural Performance in Developing Countries, *Finance and Development*, 23 (3).

Jain, L.C. (1988); Poverty, Environment and Development, *Economic and Political Weekly*, 23 (7).

Mukherjee, R. (1971); Social and Cultural Components of Society and Appraisal of Social Reality. *Economic and Political Weekly*, 26 (4).

Roy, K.C. and Sen R.K. (1991); Domestic Economic Policies and Agriculture in LDCs, in Roy, K.C., Tisdell, C.A., Sen R.K. and Alauddin, M. (ed.), *Economic Development of Poor Countries: Experience, Obstacles and Sustainability in Global Perspective*, IIDS, Calcutta.

Roy, K.C. and Tisdell, C.A (1992); *Managerial Effectiveness in the Implementation of Development*, in Roy, K.C. *et al* (ed.) Development Management and Administration: A Third World Perspective, Wiley Eastern Ltd., New Delhi.

Ray, A (1986); Trade and Pricing Policies in World Agriculture, *Finance and Development*, 23 (3).

World Bank (1991): *World Development Report*, New York: Oxford University Press.

2

Sustainability of Development: A Socio-Economic Perspective

Suhas Chandra Chakrabartty

Unlike thc post-Second World War period, when the world attention was first diverted towards the problems of development in the newly independent 'underdeveloped' countries, the most important question facing the world to-day is not whether development is possible but whether development is sustainable. The question whether development is sustainable does not arise out of any lack of demand for development. Indeed, the craze for development and material progress has always been questioned by all philosophies of the world, particularly by several Indian and Eastern philosophies. If development has anything to do with human welfare, we need particularly to-day, to take a fresh look at the teachings of these philosophies.

The problem of sustainability of development is a part of the wider ecological problems threatening life in general on the earth to-day and needs to be studied in its proper perspective. In this respect, it is a peace time question and when peace is uncertain, any discussion about it is meaningful only in a probabilistic sense.

Coming now to the economics of the question, we note that the problem facing the so-called 'developed' nations is whether economic equilibrium is possible at a positive growth rate of GDP with increases in population or whether equilibrium can be maintained only if the growth rate is zero with population remaining constant. Another much discussed possibility is the one of disaster as the economy reaches 'the limits of growth'.

The outcome depends on the extent to which the sources of pessimism as envisaged by Boulding (1984) are amenable to the laws of economics. If human motivations were economically determined, sustainability of development would have been a problem of finding necessary resources. But according to Smith and Krutilla (1984) "long-run maintenance of economic well-being with a constant or growing population, in the presence of finite natural and environmental resources, seem unwarranted based on what we know today."

Though the nature of the problem of sustainability of development differs from one country to another, the problem has special dimensions for the low income countries of the world. High and rapidly increasing populations in most low income countries, make sustenance of development extremely difficult even if all resources were renewable; but most of them are scarce in low income countries. Scarcity of non-renewable resources exacerbates the problem. Moreover, sustainability of development in the low income countries crucially depends on what happens in the developed countries.

In the "general" struggle for existence man, at first, did not seem to have any very "promising" outlook. His only initial advantage, his brain, stopped improving in genetic capacity "some 500,000 years ago (*Russell*, 1961). Human progress since that time has depended upon "acquired skills handed on by tradition and education." Even though it has continued over time, human progress has not been uniform and the advance in the last five centuries has been greater than that in all previous recorded history. One important feature of this progress is an immense diversity of incomes and living conditions of people in different parts of the world. On the one hand there are areas where the majority of the people are still fighting hard to make a living. On the other there are countries where people in general are very affluent and have not known poverty for several generations. Since the Second World War almost all of the poor countries of the world are trying to better the living conditions of their people through developmental plans. That does not mean that the so-called developed countries are sitting idle. They are also trying their best to improve their economic conditions in different ways. The growth rates in these countries are greater than those in most of the countries of the backward regions. But there are countries which were once underdeveloped, but now their growth rates are surpassing the growth rates in several so-called developed' countries. Thus, if by development we mean growth in general, then the most important question facing the world to-day is not whether development is possible, but whether development is sustainable.

The question of sustainability of development does not arise out of any lack of desire or demand for development. Indeed, one can think that once the basic amenities of life can be provided for, people would grow satisfied with their state of life and would not press for further development. But "it is a paradox that wealthy nations seem more concerned than poor with the efficiency of their economic organizations" (*Stigler, 1952, p. 2*).

From a different perspective it can be pointed out that sustainability of development is being regarded as a problem only because development by itself is held to be desirable. It is hardly being questioned that development as such may not lead to an advancement in general welfare.

Though the concept of development is more pervasive than increase in material wealth, it is primarily based on an economic interpretation of society that economic improvement holds the key to the improvement in general welfare. This search for overall improvement in materials outside self was questioned by all philosophies, particularly by several strands of Hindu philosophy, Buddhism and other Eastern philosophies. If we do not make the problem of sustainability of development synonymous with the problem of maintaining continuous improvement in general human welfare, we will have to take a fresh look at the teachings of these philosophies.

The problem involved is not merely an economic one, but is essentially ecological in character. The seriousness of the problem depends upon how we view the ecological problems. There is a tendency among economists to approach the ecological problems from an ethnocentric point of view, that the preservation of nature is beneficial for the preservation of mankind. A lack of genuine concern for the variety of life existing on the earth leads economists to view the problem as essentially a problem of finding necessary resources for development and to regard the variety of life on the earth as providing amenities for human recreation (*Peterson and Fisher, 1977, p. 681*). The problem of sustainability of development becomes all the more serious if we look at the ecological problem from a biologist's concern for "the interrelations of organisms with each other and with their environment" (*Kendeigh, 1980, p. 8*).

Sustainability of development is essentially a peace time question. War implies destruction of not only weapons, but also of resources. Though preparation for war has helped economic development in its conventional sense, destruction of non-renewable resources and ecological balances makes a mockery of any rational solution of the problem. One might share the optimism sounded by Boulding in the alleged fact that "We are now in a situation where the costs of power are much greater than the benefits. The costs of defeat are far less than the costs of war" (*Boulding, 1984*). He also sets a great store by the fact that "over a considerable part of the world there are nations between whom it [war] has been abolished."

Such presumptions are always debatable. The involved questions regarding human nature and other aspects would always leave some element of uncertainty about which "there is no scientific basis on which to form any capable probability whatever" (*Keynes, 1969*).

Before proceeding further, it can be pointed out the nature of the problem is qualitatively different in underdeveloped countries from that in the developed ones. In both the cases the problem arises not out of any lack of demand for development, but out of supply constraints. It is true that as scarcities become more and more important prices rise squeezing demand, so that what becomes important is net demand for development which is always synonymous with net demand for net investment.

It is often pointed out that the essential difference between the so-called "developed" and "underdeveloped" regions lies in the fact that while growth is endemic in developed areas, stagnation characterizes the economies of underdeveloped regions. Thus, it is maintained that an underdeveloped country would cross the threshold of underdevelopment only when it reaches a stage of self-sustained growth. From an economic point of view this difference can ultimately be traced to the existence of net investment in developed areas and its non-existence in the other areas. It was long ago pointed out by Domar that maintenance of full-employment equilibrium requires income to grow at a constant compound interest rate" (*Domar, 1946*). Using the same Keynesian tools as Domar used, it can be shown that underdevelopment can be regarded as a situation of equilibrium where net investment is zero (*Chakrabarty, 1975*).

Net investment is encouraged by population growth and technological improvements. There are reasons to believe that not only population growth and technological improvements condition the rate of economic development (*Solow, 1956; Swan, 1956*), but population growth is also influenced by economic development (*Coale and Hoover, 1958, pp. 9-17*).

The interactions between population growth, technological improvement and economic growth have always intrigued economists and sociologists to speculate about the possible sequence of industrial progress. One possibility is that there would be smooth equilibrium development with long-run adjustments between population growth and economic development (*Solow, 1956; Swan, 1956*). Another possibility is that equilibrium would eventually be reached at zero population growth and zero economic development. A third possibility is that population growth and technological improvements would generate problems of such magnitudes that human development would eventually head for a global disaster as envisaged by Meadows and others of the Club of Rome (*Meadows et. al, 1976*). In order to enquire into these possibilities we need to take into consideration several factors. We have to distinguish between development-augmenting and development-inhibiting factors on the one hand and factors which have got economic impacts but are primarily determined by non-economic considerations on the other.

We have already noted that investments encouraged by technological progress, population growth and expansion of markets are the development-augmenting forces. The development-inhibiting forces have been categorized by Boulding (*1984*) into "four major sources of pessimism in the world today". Including nuclear war, they are resource depletion, uncontrollable population increase and "system breakdowns" like the Great Depression of the 1930s and "the first collectivization of agriculture under Stalin, in which five or six million people died".

These sources of pessimism have their roots not only in the changing objective material conditions, but also in the objective human propensities. The relevant question is: how are these conditions amenable to economic laws? The prospect would have been much brighter if we could rely on an economic interpretation of history. If "the smaller costs of defeat than the costs of war" and "marketable licences to have, say, 2.2 children" as suggested by Boulding (*1984*) were successful deterrents of war and rapid population increase, we would not have much reason to worry. But wars are dictated by politicians, population growth is determined by cultural and religious sentiments and resources are used in ways where economists are hardly consulted. They are only asked to find necessary means for or work out the monetary details of ventures like "star wars" suggested by extra-economic considerations. Thus, while England waged the war, Keynes thought it to be his duty to write and suggest "How to Pay for the War."

Public sentiments against commercialization have always been quite strong. They were given the most emphatic form in the Communist Manifesto which made commercialisation of the society a byproduct of the emergence of the bourgeoisie economic system. It traced the evils of the society to the reduction of all "idyllic relationships" and "personal dignity" to "exchange value" and "crude self-interest and unfeeling cash payment" (*Ryszanoff*, 1972). Germaine Greer's *The Female Eunach* is a classic dramatisation of the state of women in a fully commercialized capitalist world (*Toynbee*, 1991).

With the passage of time, it is becoming more and more clear that the trouble lies not with commercialization as such, but with ourselves and the institutions consolidated over time. Many of these institutions and "idyllic relationships" harbour behind them systematic oppression and exploitation of the masses. Commercialization is nothing but the process of conversion of the realities in terms of money. If the realities are harsh, monetization may help to accentuate this harshness. But it helps to summarize and aggregate a variety of problems involved in terms of a single measure and thereby may make things easy for their solution by the laws of economics. The demerits that are associated with commercialization are often due to monopolization while commercialization irons out differences by letting the differences speak in terms of money. For example, in a perfectly commercialized or monetised society perfect competition will rule out differences in wages which cannot be accounted for by the differences in the nature of the work done.

But the problem is that the world is governed not by the laws of economics alone. If the laws of economics governed all aspects of human motivation, sustainability of development would have been a problem of finding necessary resources, and one might think that the laws of substitution would have taken care of that problem. For example, the laws of substitution would, perhaps, be able to solve the problem of energy, for solar energy "may become a very significant source, especially of domestic electricity, in the next few decades". But "when we come to materials, the outlook is a good deal gloomy, especially in the long run, than it is for energy" (*Boulding, 1984*). If not much material is available from outside the world in the near future, so that the earth can be considered as a spaceship, sustained life, as Robert Heilbroner points out, would require "a meticulous balance between the life-support capability of the vehicle and the demands made by the inhabitants of the craft (*Samuelson, 1980*). Moreover, if "we take as the price of a first class ticket the resource requirements of those passengers who travel in the Northern Hemisphere of the Spaceship, we have now reached a point at which the steerage is condemned to live forever...at a second class level; or at which a considerable change in living habits must be imposed on first class if the ship is ever to be converted into a one-class cruise" (*Samuelson, 1980*). Granting smooth operation of the laws of economics "confident judgements on the long-run maintenance of economic well-being with a constant or growing population in the presence of finite natural and environmental resources seem unwarranted based on what we know to-day" (*Smith and Krutilla, 1984*).

Even if we allow for sustained economic development with positive population growth and growth in construction of building and factories, we might experience a "system breakdown" through the piling up of psychological pressure on the people. The evolving situation is one consisting of many contradictions. For example, when we are forced to live with increasing number of people, we are feeling more and more isolated as we are being surrounded by more and more unknown persons. Thus, when we need to socialize' more, privatization in social and economic life is the cry of the day. This isolation of individuals from other individuals and from nature is forcing people to seek satisfaction in pathogenic consumption. For example, being totally oblivious to the needs of the downtrodden, the people who can afford are spending time in consumption to get rid of their unearned income on the one hand and to seek artificial wildness when actual wildness is vanishing quite fast on the horizon on the other. This pathogenic consumption is a boon to the producers and the businessmen, who exploit the situation with gobblesome advertisement. With his "instinct and emotion" "shaped to suit a wilder and more primitive world" man is being compressed into more organized and crowded atmosphere. Though man learnt the advantages of social co-operation, there is greater and greater pressure mounting on his nerves which may incite him to turn "the hostility and suspicion, which he had hitherto directed towards lions and tigers, upon his fellow men" (*Russell, 1961*). And as the world is getting more and more interconnected, social eruptions at one place is likely to be communicated fast to other parts of the world. It is this psychological aspect, more than the technical and economic ones, may result in a system breakdown.

The nature of the problem of sustainability of development facing the "industrial market economies" is qualitatively different from those posed by other categories of countries. Specifically, the countries of the "East European non-market economies" face a totally different situation with regard to this question, compared to the countries belonging to the categories of low income and middle income economies or high income oil exporters.

Sustainability of development in the high income oil exporting countries depends crucially on the total volume of oil reserves they command, their rates of depletion, the rates at which substitutes are being used and the nature of the cartel that they maintain. It can be expected that so long as the economic problems are well under control political developments in these countries will not lead to any system breakdown.

The middle income countries present a widely diversified economic scenario. Several of these countries have been cruising in the high and shallow waters of development, registering growth rates greater than in some industrial market economies. Diseconomies of scale have not emerged as a big problem. Thus, sustainability of development is not much of a concern to most of them.

The problem of sustainability of development assumes much more serious and interesting proportions in the East European non-market and low income economies. The breakdown of the non-market economies in the East European countries poses the serious question whether development can be sustained under a socialistic pattern of society. If one sticks to the economic interpretation of history, one might surmise that socialist revolutions were possible only where sustained developments were impossible under non-socialist economic framework of society. Thus, conversion of these countries to market economies does not guarantee sustainability of development. And this is precisely the conclusion we reached above. This oscillation of societies from market economies to non-market ones and again back to market economies has serious implications for sustainability of development. In this respect it seems worthwhile to look into the proper meaning of development which can be done only from a philosophical point of view.

The question of sustainability of development in the case of low income countries has several facets. In the first place, sustainability of development is out of question in those low income countries where the pre-conditions for take-off are still not fully developed. It can be pointed out in this respect that, notwithstanding Kuznets' criticisms of Rostow's stages theory of economic growth, these Rostowvian phrases have assumed wider connotations in which they are still meaningful. The question under our review is relevant in the case of those low income countries which have crossed over the take-off stage and are in the stage of self-sustained growth.

It is quite possible to imagine that, for the countries where self-sustained increase in GNP is quite assured, per capita GNP can be falling. The Harrodian case of the actual rate of growth being less than the population growth rate has been experienced by a number of developing countries. In many low income countries growth has been achieved with the active participation of the government in the development process. In the absence of a minimal amount of monetisation of the economy this development process has been exploited by unscrupulous business houses. The markets experienced a tortuous process of growth and the scenario is very different from that envisaged by Solow and Swan in which the "warranted rate" of growth conforms to the "natural rate" of growth. The Malthusian theory of population seems to be more relevant in these areas and population explosion has led to an alarming rate of unemployment and poverty on the one hand and increasing concentration of income in the hands of a few families on the other.

The mixed economy approach initiating development in these countries has made its own contribution towards corrupting work-ethic in the whole country in general and efficiency in public enterprises in particular. The wind of privatization that is now blowing over the whole world will certainly reduce inefficiency at large, but its impact on unemployment and inequalities in the low income countries will depend on the prevalence of several factors.

Most low income countries are poor in resources not only in absolute magnitudes but also in comparison to their populations whose big sizes pose serious problems in most low income countries. Since labour contributes to production, one might argue that high populations are big resources for growth and output can be maximised by adopting labour-intensive techniques of production. But, even neglecting the Malthusian theory of population, Galenson and Leibenstein point out that what is important for growth is the amount that can be saved and reinvested after meeting the consumption demand of the workers (*Sen, 1957*). From their point of view capital-intensive techniques would be more desirable from the long-run development point of view. But the extent to which such benefits can be utilized for development depends upon the government's efficiency to remain immune to the demands of more humane aspects of development. In most cases, the governments in such countries have to yield to political pressures which act in several ways to reduce development. Thus, big populations in low income countries can be deterrents enough for sustainance of development.

Moreover, as the initial stages of economic development under government auspices peter out and resource scarcities and diminishing returns rear their heads, the nature of labour as human capital begins to be understood. If a person's net earnings depends, as Gary Becker (*1975*) points out, upon the amount of investments made on him in the past, the low income countries, especially where "population is still largely dependent on agriculture, and the amount of new land or other resources is limited—including Bangladesh, Burundi, Egypt, India, Kenya and Nepal—progress in the face of continuing rapid population growth will be extra-ordinarily difficult" (*The World Bank, 1984*).

The costs of rapid population growth are "cumulative". "More births now make the task of slowing population growth later more difficult, as today's children become tomorrow's new parents." If appropriate population policies are not taken in time, not only "the already existing precarious balance between natural resources and people", and "the rapid growth of cities in developing countries" would be hard to manage, but per capita growth rates of income would be impossible to maintain. Inaction today "could mean that more drastic steps, less compatible with individual choice and freedom, will seem necessary tomorrow to slow population growth (*The World Bank, 1984*).

Finally, in investigating "the range of possibilities for the world economy in 1985-95", the World Bank considered two basic scenarios. "The Low case indicates what might happen if the industrial countries were to do nothing to improve their [low] performance of the past ten years." "The High case, by contrast, offers industrial economies a path of sustained and steady expansion, with GDP growing at 4.3 per cent a year in 1985-95." The difference between these two cases implies a difference between a growth rate of 5.5 per cent a year in 1985-95 and that of only 4.7 per cent a year during the same period for the developing countries. And that "would make the difference between almost every country in the world raising per capita incomes and people in many of the world's poorest countries growing steadily poorer."

"Industrial countries provide a market for about 65 per cent of the developing world's exports. Their buoyancy—or lack of it—and the amount of trade protection they choose to employ have a critical influence on the foreign exchange earning of developing countries. These earnings in turn will largely determine whether the "debt crisis" gradually subsides, or seriously retards the growth prospects of developing countries for many years to come" (*The World Bank, 1984*). In this respect the efforts for the establishment of a New International Economic Order to reorient the distribution of gains from international trade should be directed more towards an investigation of the nature of economies prevailing in the developing countries so that they do not fall a victim to the forces of monopolistic and monopsonistic influences determining the terms of trade (*Chakrabartty, 1988*).

REFERENCES

Becker, G. (1975): *Human Capital: A Theoretical and Empirical Analysis. With Special Reference to Education*, Columbia University Press.

Boulding, K.E., May (1984): Sources of Reasonable Hope for the Future. *The American Economic Review*, May.

Chakrabartty, S., July (1975): Income Determination: A Reconciliation Between Keynes and Domar, *Business Studies*, Vol. I, No. 1. University College of Business Studies, Calcutta.

Chakrabartty, S.C., (1988): *A Study in the Distribution of Gains from International Trade*, Ph. D. Dissertation, Utah State University, U.S.A.

Coale, Ansley J. and Hoover, Edger M. (1958): *Population Growth and Economic Development in Low Income Countries*, Princeton, New Jersey, Princeton University Press, pp. 9-17.

Domar, E. (1970): Capital Expansion, Rate of Growth and Employment, *in* Amartya Sen, (ed.): *Growth Economics*, Penguin Modern Economics Readings, pp. 67-68.

Kendeigh, Charles S., (1980): *Ecology with Special Reference to Animals and Man*, Prentice Hall of India Private Limited, New Delhi.

Keynes, J.M. (1969): The General Theory of Employment, Quarterly Journal of Economics, *in* R.W. Clower, (ed.): *Monetary Theory*, Penguin Modern Economics Readings, p. 217.

Meadows, D.H., *et al.* (1975): *The Limits to Growth*, A Potomac Associates Book, Pan Books, London and Sydney.

Myrdal, Gunnar (1971): *The Challenge of World Poverty*, A Penguin International Edition.

Peterson, F.M. and Fisher, A.C. (1977): The Exploitation of Extractive Resources: A Survey, *The Economic Journal*, December.

Ryszanoff, D. (1972): *The Communist Manifesto of Karl Marx and Friedrich Engels*, Radical Book Club, Calcutta, pp. 28-29.

Samuelson, Paul A. (1980): *Economics*, Eleventh Edition, p. 750.

Sen, A. (1970): *Growth Economics*, Penguin Modern Economics Readings, Penguin Books, pp. 20-30.

Sen, Amartya K., (1957): Some Notes on the Choice of Capital-Intensity in Development Planning, *The Quarterly Journal of Economics*, Vol. LXXI, November.

Smith, V.K. and Krutilla, John V. (1984): Economic Growth, Resource Availability, and Environmental Quality, *American Economic Review*, May.

Solow R.M. (1956): A Contribution to the Theory of Economic Growth, *Quarterly Journal of Economics*, Vol. 70, pp. 65-94.

Stigler, George J. (1952): *The Theory of Price*, Revised Editon, The Macmillan Company, New York, p. 2.

Swan, T.W. (1956): Economic Growth and Capital Accumulation, *Economic Record*, Vol. 32.

Toynbee, P. (1991): A Woman's Work is Never Done, *The Statesman*, Calcutta, October 13.

World Bank (1984): *World Development Report*, Oxford University Press, pp. 1,2, 8-9, 34-35.

3

Sustainability of Development for LIEs and Economic Agenda for the 1990s and Beyond

Raj Kumar Sen

The concepts of development and its sustainability are found to be changing over time and among countries. These are to be determined as functions of not only region-specific economic and other resources but also of many non-quantifiable factors like social norms and ethical values. In view of the experiences of the low income economies (LIEs) during the last few decades, it is now clear that unidirectional and materialistic growth strategies—whether they are operating under market-oriented mixed economies or collectivist command economies cannot be allowed to dominate their policy-making any more.

While both unbridled competition, and totalitarian controls are found to lead the economies in a state of non-sustainable disequilibrium, it is high time that the policy-makers of the LIEs go for experimenting with alternative development strategies preached by Schultz, Myrdal, Schumacher, Gandhi and others in a holistic, decentralised and integrated manner with due concern for the overall environment and welfare of the common people, the upliftment of which happened to be the declared focal point of all development strategies. However, the modem craze of the policy-makers of many LIEs to imitate blindly the consumerist economic strategies of the industrialised high income economies in spite of the formers' awareness about their unsustainable nature in their context, may lead in the 1990s to further deterioration of the situation in those LIEs which are particularly overburdened with high population growth and mass poverty. Only an enlightened and liberal world opinion free from dogma can effectively reformulate the economic agenda of the LIEs for the 1990s and beyond in a sustainable manner.

While the aim for achieving individual and social prosperity perpetually allured human activities and influenced state policies, the concern for development in economic thinking is one of recent origin. Since the days of near universal acceptance of GNP as the kingpin of macro-policies targetting at the enhancement of wealth of nations and the growth of utilitarian analysis of the behaviour of the economic agents of the society, the seeds of growth economics were sown in economic literature. They germinated in the form of development economics since the forties of the present century when in his seminal work[1], Clark drew the attention of the world to the massive per capita income differences that existed between countries and provided the empirical impetus for the study of the underdeveloped—in fact, low income economies as a separate branch of economics as a subject.

Of course it is well-known that with the Keynesian revolution the emphasis of economic discussion shifted from the neo-classical partial equilibrium framework to a general equilibrium one and the possibility of a multiplied amount of increase in income through additional public autonomous investment actually guided[2] the growth economists to divide the world into developed and underdeveloped regions primarily on the basis of differences in per capita income or GDP (in the line of the analysis by Clark) and many other associated features characterising an underdeveloped economy.[3] But these other associated features of underdevelopment are always made secondary and/or function of primarily income only exactly in the same manner in which utility maximisation has been made the sole target for a consumer (through consumption of economic goods only) while the most important propagator of the utility calculus *viz.*, Marshall pointed out clearly that "the progressive nature of man is one whole" and "it is only temporarily and provisionally that we can with profit isolate for study the economic side of his life."[4] Concentrating thus on national income mainly in the macro-front and on maximisation of consumption in the micro-behaviour, the general trend of growth economics has been so far to augment to growth of the GDP of an economy with the expectation that it will take care of all other factors. In particular, the industrialisation process (with the neo-classical production function at the heart of its analysis) was considered to be the engine of growth. Economic development was considered at that time synonymous with economic growth and trust was placed in the trickle down theory of benefits to the masses and in particular, to the weaker sections of the population.

However, the experiences of the low income economies (LIEs) proved beyond doubt that the neo-classical theory of growth (including the long-term one as devised by Solow in the 1950s) has been found to be patently inadequate to explain the varying performances of their growth strategies. The high income economies also have been no exception in this field. We observe that the economies of Japan, Korea, Taiwan and other Asian dragons expanded at an astonishing pace in the last four decades while much of Africa has stagnated or declined. In the last twenty years, the growth of productivity slowed in America. With their huge population and natural resources India and China could hardly uplift their positions in the income ranking of different countries. With the assumptions of constant returns to scale and perfect competition, the neo-classical theory in fact could not explain why for today's industrial countries, the returns to investment have been higher in the past few decades than they were in the late 19th and early 20th century. Similarly the facts for the world barring the high income countries and the Asian dragons do not corroborate the neo-classical implication that the poor countries should find it easy to grow much faster than rich ones as investment in a country with little capital should spur output more powerfully than a proportionate amount of investment in a country with plenty. A study of 114 countries in 1988 by Summers and Heston[5] on their annual GDP growth during 1960-85 demonstrated just the opposite. Of course the fact of differences in the rates of flow of new technology in different groups of countries has been forwarded to find answers to such uncomfortable situations. But even then, while debate on the extent of contribution of technical progress to economic growth continues, statistical tests prove that technological progress is simply the residual—the thing that accounts for any growth that cannot be accounted for in other ways.

An analysis of the World Bank's notion about the decade of eighties as a "lost decade" for the low-income economies shows more clearly the failure of the mainstream growth-*cum*-development economics. In spite of the fact that the real per capita income grew and poverty declined in South and in particular, East Asia, in countries of Latin America and Sub-Saharan Africa, real per capita income, living standards and investment have slipped. At the end of the decade, the World Bank estimated that out of a world population of nearly 5284 millions, a population of about 3058 million (approximately 58 per cent) lived with a meagre income of US $ 610 or less. Again a sizeable amount of 1133 million people in all developing countries or 29.7 per cent of their population had been under the poverty line in 1990. It may be pointed out at this stage that the Bank itself has discontinued its grouping of countries as developing economies since its 1989 Report. Currently it mentions that "low-income and middle-income economies are sometimes referred to as developing economies". This is done as "the use of the term is convenient; it is not intended to imply that all economies in the group are experiencing similar development or that other economies have reached a preferred or final stage of development." Hence, it concludes that "classification by income does not necessarily reflect development status". But still for operational and analytical purposes, the World Bank's main criterion for developing economies by their per capita GNP at constant prices (US dollars) has to be continued though there are many attempts to construct various development indicators in one way or other to present the development scenario of countries in a more accurate manner.

However, it has long been recognised that per capita income or GDP as a measure of development is not able to capture all dimensions of economic well-being of the individual and the society, though income has been used as a measure of economic welfare for a long time and in particular since Pigou[6] defined economic welfare in 1932 as that part of social welfare that can be "brought directly or indirectly into relation with the measuring rod of money". In fact it cannot be denied that the issues of non-marketed goods (like household production, externalities such as pollution and environmental degradation etc.), impacts of human effort necessary to produce outputs (and also of leisure) and inclusion of regrettable necessities[7] like defence and police expenditures etc., all affecting the quality of life, social justice etc., are commonly regarded as deficiencies of the national accounting process followed by countries in the measurement of their national incomes. Various attempts have been made to capture these dimensions by adjusting the GDP in various ways and other methods. More important and well famous of such attempts are the Nordhaus-Tobin measure (1972) of net economic welfare (NEW), Economic aspects of Welfare (ISEW) by Daly and Cobb (1989) etc. The World Bank methodology for computing internationally comparable per capita national income (Altas Methodology) has also been sought to be improved in UN International Comparison Project (1968) resulting into the Penn World Tables enabling real quantity comparisons to be made both over time and between countries. But more attention is now diverted to measure levels of living[8] enjoyed by people in different countries. These measures attempt to consider socio-economic development, index for physical quality of life (PQLI) (based on infant mortality, life expectancy, literacy), weighted index of social progress (WISP) and Human Development Index (HDI) (devised by the United Nations Development Programme and based on life expectancy, literacy and per capita income) and others focusing on issues other than income either excluding or including income as one of its determining factors. But all such attempts have not yet been able to persuade the policymakers of low-income economies to modify their income-augmenting strategies adopted in the name of economic development to an appreciable extent. There has been of course a widespread concern for protection of environment and ecology in recent times (specially since the 1972 Stockholm Conference and accelerated during the eighties) but it is not realised properly that environmental degradation is mostly the consequence of following materialistic growth strategy unmindful of their non-economic repurcussions on the society at large. This is clearly visible when we note that the World Bank has prescribed an alternative path to allow the coming generation to witness improved environmental conditions accompanied by rapid economic development and the virtual eradication of widespread poverty and in doing so, it has suggested to take advantage of the positive links between economic efficiency, income growth and protection of the environment,[9] thus helping to identify the diseconomies resulted from pursuing the conventional income-augmenting policies by the authorities of the affected economies.

The inefficacy of such policies in augmenting their incomes even is amply demonstrated in a study[10] of the LIEs in 1980 and 1987 on the basis of the relevant World Development Reports. It is well known that the LIEs follow their income-oriented growth policies on the expectation to bridge their gap with the rich countries as quickly as possible. Naturally we may be interested in the fact that how far the LIEs as a country group could uplift their income levels into the next higher income group *i.e.*, the lower middle income one. It has been observed that the number of LIEs being 33 in 1980, increased to 42 in 1987 as nine countries belonging to the lower middle income group actually slipped into the LIE group in this period. This finding goes completely against their expectation as they were totally unable to move into the next higher income group. The situation has not improved in 1990 also as the number of LIEs in that year stood at 43. It goes without saying that when the LIEs are unable to raise their group income, the trickle-down theory of benefits to the downtrodden from the growth of the GDP can be best defined in the words of Galbraith (as he has done in his book, *The Culture of Contentment*) that "if one feeds the horse enough oats, some will pass through the road for the sparrows." It is really strange that even this revelation of the failure of conventional growth economics has not motivated the LIEs adequately to seriously search for an alternative development paradigm.

Not only the failure to raise the income level of the group as a whole, but also the near-constancy of the inter-country development scenario of the LIEs in this period in spite of their development efforts has been revealed empirically in this study for a sample of 26 economies with available comparable data, in terms of development indicators like density of population, infant mortality rate, life expectancy at birth and daily per capita calorie supply including the per capita GNP. On the basis of calculated rank correlation coefficients for each indicator for two points of time *viz.* 1980 and 1986, it has been observed that there has been an overall consistency for all of them between the rank orders of the two years. This implied that the relative position of the LIEs so far as their level of development is concerned, has not changed substantially during this period. This consistency in rank correlation coefficient is highest for density of population indicating the ineffectiveness of the growth strategies to influence the density of population of these economies. There has also been no major change in the inter-country ordering of the per capita GDP level showing the relative ineffectiveness of different brands of growth strategies followed by the respective LIEs in changing appreciably even their rankings among themselves. The position of health care has been already very alarming in the LIEs in terms of the infant mortality rate as this variable also behaved in an unchanged manner in this period of reference. For the remaining two development indicators enquired in this study, it is observed that while life expectancy of these economies have gone up in this period (mainly as a result of invention of life saving drugs rather than due to more health care facilities provided as a part of adopted growth strategies), no conclusive evidence could be derived for an increase in the daily per capita intake of calorie for the sample LIEs during the period of reference.

Contrary to our common belief, it has been also found in this study through linear regression coefficients that individually the selected development indicators in the sample LIEs did not depend on the level of income in a statistically significant manner during the period under study. Thus, while the LIEs are increasing their individual GNP levels (through adopted economic policies), they are unable to enhance the quality of life of their people in general through this growth of income. All these finding repeatedly show the need to follow an alternative strategy of development for the LIEs in a non-conventional manner. For this objective, geographical, regional, climatic and other relevant conditions including the non-economic ones (*e.g.*, ethical, political, sociological etc.) must be taken into account to construct an appropriate development model for individual LIEs. It should be noted that in order to be a sustainable one, development models should be constructed for individual countries with due weightage given to every member's random components and requirements. It is now well-known that a mere materialistic approach towards development has proved to be quite inadequate and ineffective for the LIEs. The emphasis should shift from a quantitative account of growth to a more cautious analysis to the content of it with special emphasis to the human resource development and upliftment of the quality of life.

The alternative growth path to the mixed economy type of growth policy has been the prescription of socialism for the LIEs specially since the end of the Second World War. But the experiences of the former USSR and the East European countries following the so-called socialist path as revealed in the period of confluence between the decades of eighties and nineties clearly prove the unsustainable nature of growth along the socialist path too. It may be noted that while the socialist strategies of growth are totally in opposition to the market based ones, both of them pursued a materialistic policy for the economic growth of their countries. In one sense the socialist countries emphasised on the material aspects of the economy more than others through their concentration on the maximisation of the gross material product. It is now further revealed that while the USSR alone achieved some form of military supremacy, none of the economies belonging to this group could attain the economic prosperity of the industrialised West. The much publicised success stories of these economies in the provision of basic needs to everyone even at the cost of freedom enjoyed by the people in the countries which were rich but featured unequal distribution of income and wealth are now found to be either untrue or impossible to continue for long. Such misinformations about the economic conditions of the erstwhile socialist economies including the former USSR, have done enormous harm in moulding the economic policies of the LIEs aimed towards their economic growth with a socialist bias and market bashing attributes. Long decades of ineffective and fruitless public controls have now resulted in world reaction which has swung the economic pendulum in the opposite extreme of privatisation and economic liberalisation. In their present craze to reduce the public sector and its responsibilities, the LIEs are now forgetting the fact that it is not possible to optimise the returns from allocation of resources when the competition is not a perfect one and at least in the spheres[11] of health, education and social security, the private sector cannot assume the responsibility of the state authority as the returns from these sectors are extremely unremunerative. It appears that the LIEs are running between alternative growth paths all of which lead to unsustainable disequilibrium.

What is strange and rather disturbing in this context is the fact that the truly sustainable alternative path to economic development is neither unknown nor unattainable. In reality quite a few authorities have registered their objections against the conventional growth strategies emphasising the quantitative aspects only of the various indicators of economic development. For instance[12] the question of income distribution has been considered to be logically more important than that of the ideal output by Little. Mishan argued that once subsistence levels are exceeded, the possession of more goods is neither the sole nor the chief source of men's satisfaction. He further commented that the technical means designed to pursue further material ends may produce a civilisation "uncongenial to the psychic needs of ordinary men." Arrow is also not willing to attach any significance to the quantity of output which is neutral to its distribution. Dobb wanted to attach equal weightage to production and distribution of output as factors affecting the level of welfare of the society. Lewis and Nurkse emphasised on the dualities and disguised unemployment existing in LIEs and for them they opined for the need of a balanced growth strategy. The importance of human capital rather than the physical capital has been emphasised by Schultz as not space, energy, cropland or other physical properties of the earth, but this resource is decisive in improving the welfare of the poor people throughout the world. Hla Myint could realise that "in practice there is a real danger of macromodels of economic development running on their own steam without any reference to the fundamental human problems of backwardness on the subjective side."

It appears that we have not paid any attention to the opinion of Gunnar Myrdal who was vocal about the limitations of the growth theories immitated from the Western economies for their fruitful application in the LIEs. He did not accept the definition of development itself in terms of growth only and he preferred the implementation of income equalisation measures to a just quantitative increase in the GDP specially for countries suffering from acute poverty and highly skew income distribution. So far as countries like India are concerned, the institutionalist approach of Myrdal was advocated long ago by M.K. Gandhi[13] when he advocated to use more of current economy resources for the purpose of economic activities as these are with relatively unlimited stocks and less of reservoir economy with limited stocks. His economics centred around the concept of the 'whole man' instead of the concern of the conventional economics about the 'economic man'. He conceived the development process in a totally different manner through his idea of self-reliant village economy which had been the traditional feature of India till the advent of the British rule. He never accepted growth for the sake of growth only in materialistic terms and always upheld the objective of upliftment of the 'man' himself with special emphasis to *antyodaya i.e.,* the upliftment of the weakest one. Considering the unique and special features, resources and potentials of individual countries and regions, Gandhi relied on a policy of decentralisation in its true sense.

Of course the awareness about these alternative approaches is also traceable in varying degrees in recent times in many contributions to economic literature[14] and institutional approaches. Amartya Sen has called for enhancing human potential where economic development may be conceived as the process of expanding capabilities of the people which ultimately leads to the expansion of their entitlement. Schumacher also echoed the Gandhian prescription of consumption planning and the vital need for humanistic approach to economic growth of the LIEs. Since 1990, the World Bank has devoted its annual World Development Reports successively to central themes like 'poverty', the 'challenge of development' and 'development and environment' respectively clearly revealing its shifting focus on world issues. The Human Development Index mentioned earlier is now providing an alternative ranking of the economies by the UNDP.

In India, one of the largest LIEs in the world, the wage-goods model was prescribed in the fifties as a more appropriate growth strategy compared with the adopted Mahalanobis model as the former was targeted to the supply of mass consumption goods to the people. With the passage of time, the economic planning based on centralised, unbalanced and heavy industry-oriented capital-intensive strategy, has failed in India to deliver the goods and/or reduce the poverty[15] (which has the highest concentration in South Asia and India in particular) appreciably. The planning results gradually exhibited some features of maldevelopment while many attributes of underdevelopment[16] like high rate of population growth, excessive dependence of agriculture, low per capita availability of mass consumption goods, excessive inequality in the distribution of income with increasing consumption dualism and conspicuous consumption, mass poverty and unemployment, growing dependence on indirect tax etc. continued to prevail in a significant scale even after several decades. Naturally, when it was felt that a minimum level of living must be provided for all, the objective of poverty removal came in the forefront and poverty alleviation measures occupied important places since the Fifth Five Year Plan though these measures were not properly integrated with the planning framework and nor the basic planning strategy was changed. However, acute imbalances in the balance of payments front and growing concerns about environmental[17] degradation as a result of growth strategies have recently prompted the authorities to go for market-friendly strategies and reduction of the public sector responsibilities. The new Eighth Plan also put great emphasis on human resource development and declared to take care of many fronts hitherto neglected.

But all these measures adopted in India and many other LIEs do not promise high hopes for these economies for a sustainable development in the 1990s and beyond. It should be remembered that mere tinkering with the alternative development strategies which are holistic, decentralised and integrated with due concern for the overall environment and welfare of the common people, cannot produce the desired results. The modern craze of the policy-makers of many LIEs to imitate blindly the consumerist economic strategies of the industrialised high income economies in spite of the former's awareness about their unsustainable nature in their context may lead in the 1990s to further deterioration of the situation specially in those LIEs which are overburdened with high population growth and widespread poverty. The root cause of such possibilities however actually lie in the political economy[18] of development paradigms in the LIEs including India. We are aware that the western growth strategies exported to the LIEs of the East served indirectly at least three significant political objectives of the rich countries. These were respectively to provide a viable alternative to the Soviet model for the newly independent countries, to retain an economic control on such countries through the policy of condition-tied loans in the name of foreign aid and finally to capture the huge markets of such overpopulated countries. The recent policies of the IMF, World Bank, GATT and other international financial agencies and the lending countries bear ample evidences of such observations. The decades of experiments with unsustainable growth strategies have also led to the creation of centres of entrenched vested interests in the LIEs who are against the overall change of the current policies to a truly alternative and sustainable one. Only an enlightened and liberal world opinion free from political and economic dogma can effectively reformulate the economic agenda of the LIEs for the 1990s and beyond in a sustainable manner. The darkness of hedonism may appear to be too deep to overcome when economics is artificially divorced from ethics and human values are influenced by uncontrolled consumption and income. But, if we can be firm in strengthening the positive symptoms appearing all over the world and courageously press to follow the optimum strategies, the dawn is sure to come.

REFERENCES

1. Clark, C.G. (1940): *The Conditions of Economic Progress*. Macmillan.
2. Sen, Raj Kumar and Roy, K.C. (1990): Utility, Marshall and Development Economics. *Indian Economic Conference Papers*, Muzaffarpur.
3. Arndt, H. (1990): Colin Clark as a Development Economist—*World Development*. Vol 18. No. 7.
4. Marshall, A. (1962): *Principles of Economics*. 8th Ed. ELBS, London.
5. Summers, R. and Heston, A. (1992): A New Set of International Comparisons of Real Product and Price Levels: Estimates for 130 countries. 1950-1985. *Review of Income and Wealth*. Series 34, No. 1. 1988 (Reported in *The Economic Times*, 13 January, as "The Old Order Changeth").
6. Pigou, A.C. (1932): *The Economics of Welfare*. Macmillan, London.
7. Doessel, D.P. and Gounder, Rukmani (1992): International Comparisons of Levels of Living and the Human Development Index: Some Empirical Results. First IIDS Conference on Development and Future Studies Papers, Calcutta.
8. Ekins, P. (1990): An Indicator Framework for Economic Progress. *Development*. No. 3-4.
9. World Bank (1992): *op cit*.
10. Sen, Raj Kumar and Dasgupta, M.K. (1989): The Development Scenario of the Low Income Economies in the Eighties. An Empirical Evaluation. *Indian Econometric Conference Papers*. Bangalore.
11. Sen, Amartya (1992): Socialism, Markets and Democracy *in* Sen, Raj Kumar (ed.): *From Diamond to Platinum: IEA Presidential Addresses 1977-91*. IEA Trust for R & D and IIDS.
12. Little, I.M.D.: *A Critique of Welfare Economics*, Oxford University Press. UK. 1960; Arrow, K.J.: *Social Choice and Individual Values*. J. Wiley and Sons. N. York; Dobb. M.: *Welfare Economics and the Economics of Socialism*. Cambridge University Press, 1969, Schultz, T.W.,: *Investing in People*. Hindusthan Publishing Corporation. Delhi 1981; Myint, H.: *An Interpretation of Economic Growth*. Gandhian Institute of Studies. Varanasi 1962: Mishan, R.J.: *Welfare Economics: An Assessment*. North Holland Publishing Co. 1969.
13. Sen, R.K. (1985): Level of Living ana Gaudhian Economic Theory in the Indian Planning, *Indian Economic Conference Volume*. Ahmedabad, India.

14. Sen, Amartya: *Commodities and Capabilities*. Oxford University Press. Delhi 1987; Schumacher, E.F.: *Roots of Economic Growth*. Gandhian Institute of Studies. Varanasi 1962; World Bank: *op. cit.* 1990, 1991 (The Challenge of Development), 1992.

15. Sen, Raj Kumar (1991): Development and Poverty Alleviation with reference to India: A Quest for Policies, *in* Roy, K.C., Tisdell, C.A., Sen, R.K. and Alauddin, M. (ed.): *Economic Development of Poor Countries: Experiences, Obstacles and Sustainability in Global Perspective*. International Institute for Development Studies, Calcutta.

16. _____ (1968): Planning for Indian Economic Development. *Society and Change*. New Delhi, March.

17. _____ (1992): India's Economic Growth: How Far it has been Environment-Friendly *in* Roy, K.C., Tisdell, C.A., Sen, R.K. (ed.) ; *Economic Development and Environment: A case study of India*. Oxford University Press, Calcutta.

18. Sen, Raj Kumar (1995): Political Economy of Development Paradigms in LDCs with reference to India in Gupta, K.R. (ed.) *Issues in Indian Economy*, Vol. I, Atlantic Publishers and Distributors, New Delhi.

4

Towards Sustainable Development

Veena Devasthali

The objective of this paper is to understand the meaning of 'sustainable development' and the process accompanying it. This has been attempted from the point of view of Third World countries in general and India in particular.

World Bank's World Development Report, 1988 provides a comprehensive picture of the gap that exists among the rich and poor countries. This necessitates one to rethink on the development strategy implemented so far. The experience of the developing countries indicates that the developmental model based on the experience of developed countries may bring about some increase in the quantitative indicators. However, it has failed to create livelihood opportunities for the majority. Several bottlenecks and imbalances have developed as a result of this strategy. What is required is the strategy which will be an equitable, sustainable and an environment-oriented one. Such a strategy should evolve from below with equal participation of people at the grassroot level, voluntary organisations working with them and the government officials. Women should be considered an integral part of this process from decision-making to the actual implementation and should equally share gains of development. It is only after initiating this process that a micro-macro linkage may be worked out facilitating a transition from a rural agricultural to a rural industrial economy.

The development experience of the Third World countries is reviewed briefly. This is followed by the development experience of Indian economy with a focus on the emerging bottlenecks, during the process of development. Last, need for the search for alternatives and a few alternatives which are being explored presently are discussed in the context of substainable development.

Each passing day is bringing the year 2000 A.D. closer. It not only marks the end of a decade but the end of a century and a millenium as well, There has been a growing need to rethink on the process of development followed so far in both the developed and the developing countries, especially in the context of the newly emerging global economic order. At this juncture, it would be useful to take stock of the experiences gathered from the development strategy followed so far.

Development economics as a branch of mainstream economics emerged in 1950s. The end of Second World War necessitated restructuring of war-torn European economies. Also several countries in Asia, Africa and Caribbean gained independence during mid-1940s to mid-1960s. Another notable event of this period was Chinese revolution. The need for initiating the process of development in the former colonial countries gave a boost to the debate on development. The paths chosen by these countries were diverse in nature and the pace of their achievements too differed from each other.

Several changes have taken place during the last half century. Especially momentous are the events of the last decade. These include the collapse of communism in eastern Europe and the disintegration of the former USSR, German unification and the reversal in America's position from the largest creditor to the largest debtor country in the world. Changes are taking place in other European countries as well.

From the point of view of developing countries we find, that the problem of underdevelopment has persisted in these countries. The inequalities between the developed and the developing countries have increased during this period. Though some quantitative achievements have been recorded in developing countries, equally glaring is the fact that the majority sections of the population in these countries are still deprived of basic necessities and means of livelihood. 1980s is the lost decade for these countries (*WDR, 1990*). The developed countries are not free from the crisis either. Among various manifestations of this crisis, one of the most important one is the increasing threat to the environment.

This brings us to the question of sustainability of development strategy which has been practised so far. Not only that the strategy has failed to bring about equity, there is also a growing danger in the form of sustainability of the entire process. It is necessary to reorient the development theory which will incorporate the relevance of diverse indigenous cultures of the developing economies and the local participation of resource base from planning to implementation. There is also a need to focus upon the so far neglected gender dimension of development.

The present paper attempts to raise these issues. Broad changes in the development thinking have been reviewed briefly in Section I. Section II deals with the development experience of the Indian economy in the post-independence period. Section III focuses upon the alternative strategy of development which will be both more equitable and sustainable. Concluding observations are summarised in Section IV.

I

Development theory as a branch of economic theory emerged in the later half of the present century. During 1950s and 1960s several developments took place in the theory. As mentioned earlier, the end of colonialism and the initiating of the development process in the newly independent colonial countries gave a tremendous boost to the development theorists. They included Lewis, Nurkse, Rosenstein Rodan and so on. Various theories emerged during this period, *viz.* 'stages of growth, 'take-off, 'dual economy model', 'capital goods' and 'wage goods model' and so on.

However, after 1960s, the theory has been on the decline. The idealism and concern about the global growth in 1950s and 1960s vanished in economically turbulent years of 1970s and 1980s (*Sen, Pranab, 1991*). This decline in theory was mainly due to the general apathy and not the hostility towards macroeconomics. According to the critics the theory fails to provide (put in stronger terms, can't provide) micro foundations in terms of the rational behaviour of individual decision-makers and also therefore of markets (*Bharadwaj, K., 1990*). Macroeconomic analysis is being increasingly challenged in developing countries. In academic economics, we find growth and development being replaced by 'stabilisation and adjustment' (*Sen, Pranab, 1991*). Another contributory factor to the increasing drive towards market economy is the events that have taken place in former USSR and eastern European countries.

However, there is a countering view; 'while macroeconomic policies and planning system are under critical fire and their complexity and operational vulnerability being vigorously attacked, critics appear to have failed to appreciate that the 'market' credited with efficiency in theory is as much an abstract paradigmatic construction of theory and the markets in reality do not conform to the manner of their functioning presumed in theory' (*Bharadwaj, K., 1990*).

Despite the changes in development thinking, from the point of view of developing countries, the fact remains that the problem of underdevelopment persists. The following section briefly reviews the development experience of Indian economy in the post-independence period. This review will be useful in formulating the alternative strategy for development.

II

The development programme in India was initiated with the launching of the First Five Year Plan in 1950-51. This period also coincided with the emergence of the development theory. The only other model available for the planners at that time was that of USSR. This historical review of the four decades of the development experience will enable in understanding the linkage between the process and the policies implemented and the constraints that have emerged during this period.

India's development strategy was formulated in a fairly comprehensive manner in the First and the Second Five Year Plans. It was a challenge to the planners to formulate a strategy which would break away from the colonial past and rise to the expectations of the newly independent nation (*Sen, Pranab, 1991*). Based on Mahalanobis model, the Planning Commission emphasized the role of capital accumulation as the main constraint facing the Indian economy. It was felt that the promotion of heavy industries will help in increasing the rate of savings. The Indian industry being in its infant stages, neither the industrial exports were expected to increase in a short period nor was the traditional export base sufficient to increase at a fast rate. The strategy of import substitution under the protection from foreign competition was the hallmark of the growing Indian industry. In order to bring about an efficient and balanced use of resources, the Industrial Policy Resolution, 1956 emphasized the role of licensing policy. The strategy of heavy industries necessitated an increasing role for the public sector. This, in short, was the development strategy followed in the initial years.

This strategy has brought about some positive results. Some quantitative achievements have been recorded during this period. Industrial production expanded. The range of products was fairly diversified. The savings constraint eased to some extent during this period. But, contrary to expectations, employment levels failed to rise along with the rising production in the manufacturing sector. There were huge cost escalating delays in the completion of several projects which further increased the burden on the economy. Especially crucial was the foreign exchange constraint during this period.

Another constraint, which was not recognised fully was that of agrarian constraint. According to Sen (*1988*), by 1960 itself, *i.e.* in the very first decade of the development programme, the agrarian constraint was operational. Despite this, the corresponding change in the policy did not take place initially due to liberal food aid which was available till 1965. Two wars during this period and the severe droughts made it necessary to rethink about the self-sufficiency in agricultural sector. The policy of Green Revolution, which was implemented as a solution to this constraint only brought about an increase in the production of selected commodities in selected regions while having no noticeable impact on the growth rate of the economy as a whole. It further accentuated the inequalities within rural areas.

The next decade of development process, *i.e.* 1970s witnessed even more turbulence than the previous decade. This decade began with the Bangladesh war in 1971. Soon followed the first oil crisis of 1973. The mounting economic crisis was accompanied by serious political crisis. The successive events included the declaration of emergency, the first non-Congress government at the Centre in 1977, the fall of Janata government and re-emergence of Congress at the centre in 1980. By the end of the decade the second oil crisis hit the economy in 1979-80. All these events contributed to the adverse impact on the economy.

Import liberalisation policies were initiated at the beginning of the next decade *i.e.* 1980s and were continued at a much more rapid pace from mid-1980s. The constraint of widening budgetary gap was added to that of foreign exchange constraint.

This brief historical sketch of India's economic transformation presents a very dismal picture. There has been an obvious failure of trickle down approach nor have the welfare schemes indicated any positive results. Therefore, what is needed is the complete re-evaluation of policies implemented so far and a simultaneous search for the new alternative strategy.

III

Search for the new strategy for development is being felt at the global as well as national level. The major issue questioning the developmental strategy in the industrially advanced countries so far is the increasing threat to the environment. The degradation of resource base is threatening the sustainability of the development model in these countries. The problem is especially acute in the developing countries because the vast majority in these countries are being increasingly deprived of their livelihood opportunities. The disillusionment towards the policies imposed by the international financial institutions has been gradually increasing (*South Commission*). The grassroot level organisations in developing countries have started raising the fundamental questions regarding the meaning and content of development.

The brief historical review of Indian economy indicates a similar picture. Although some quantitative achievements have been recorded, these have not been accompanied by the changes on the distribution front. This period has been characterized by increasing inequalities at various levels.

Since majority of the population is still dependent on the agricultural sector for their livelihood, it is necessary to take a closer look at this sector. One of the main challenges facing the agricultural sector and in turn the Indian economy is the development of dry regions. Nearly 70 per cent of the cultivated land in India is dry land; however its contribution to agricultural production is 42 per cent (*Vyasulu, V. & Others, 1991*).

The post-independence history of irrigation policy indicates, that although the irrigation and power were considered as priority areas in Five Year Plans, there has not been much change on this front. According to Five Year Plans, even after the realisation of full irrigation potential, only one-third of the area of the country can be brought under irrigation. In other words, given the accepted technological framework in the Plans, the remaining two-third of the land and thereby people dependent on this land will continue to depend on monsoon.

Thus, the development process initiated so far has failed to create livelihood opportunities for rural as well as urban poor. The carrying capacity of the degraded rural eco-system being insufficient to meet even the bare subsistence needs of rural population, they have no alternative but to migrate to urban areas seasonally, or temporarily (*Datye & Paranjape, 1990*).

Clearly, there is an urgent need for a new approach towards development strategy which will incorporate the objectives of equality and sustainability along with the increase in productivity. The focus of this strategy, in the Indian context will have to be on the solution to the problem of dry regions. As seen earlier, the major and medium irrigation projects have failed to bring about an increase in the area under irrigation, Hence, the focus of the new strategy has to be on the creation of water resources at the village level itself. This alternative approach has been provided by the watershed development programme. Various experiments are being carried out in the implementation of watershed development programmes in different parts of India. These experiments *i.e.*, those at Ralegan Siddhi, Naigaon, Ambejogai and other areas highlight certain crucial aspects of these programmes which can provide the basis for the alternative strategy for development.

In case of most of the experiments the initiative has been taken either by individuals or by some voluntary development organisations. Taking village as a unit, the programme focuses upon the storing and conserving of water at the village level itself. Although the initiative has come from individuals or the organisations, the programme, wherever it is being implemented is a participatory programme from planning till implementation of the same. The creation of vegetative cover is an important and a crucial integral aspect of the programme. The priority is given to the solution of drinking water problem, stabilization of kharif crop and the providing of fuel and fodder requirements. There is no cultivation of cash crops which require massive water inputs. The programme focuses on the creation of additional water resources and includes the proper allocation of the resources especially among the landless and the marginal farmers. The programme has evolved through the participation at grassroot level at every stage. Another notable feature is that there is almost no displacement through this programme. In short, it has all the potential of transforming the rural economy.

There has been some attempts to provide the theoretical formulation for these still isolated examples (*Datye, Joy and Patankar*). Taking these experiences as the starting point, there have been continuous attempts to explore wider implications of these programmes at micro and macro levels. What is significant is that such an approach is evolving out of continuous discussions that have been going on among social activists, technologists and social scientists? A model has been evolved through the joint interaction of various voluntary/development organizations, *viz*. CASAD, Mukti Sangharsh, Prayag Parivar and others (*Datye and Paranjape, 1990*). The salient features of this newly emerging approach based on the examples of watershed development programmes have been briefly summarized here.

Although to begin with the watershed development programme emerged as a solution to drought prone areas, it has a wider applicability to a wide range of agroclimatic and social situations. The major constraint to the development activity in rural areas is the uneven distribution of productive assets, mainly land. Therefore, the focus of the new strategy should be in the creation of new assets—*e.g.*, water, turning of wastelands of various categories into assets and so on. In this context, the concept of a group right to additional water (being provided by watershed development programme) has emerged, which focuses on the separation of water rights from ownership rights in land. Other aspects of the programme include the creation of fodder and fuel pool, establishment of a grain bank, exploring various ways to increase the bio-mass productivity and a continuous generation of on-farm and non-farm employment. It is expected that the redistribution of present assets, creation of new productive assets, prioritisation of their allocation should be brought about by the participation at the grassroot level.

The programme certainly has tremendous potential to bring about the transformation of rural economy.

Various important points emerge from this. It is significant to note from both the micro and marco point of view that a new approach towards micro planning is gradually emerging. Contrary to previous experience of developmental planning (reflected *e.g.*, in the strategy of Five Year Plans) this approach is not the one to be fitted into the broader macro framework, but the one developed as a micro-macro linkage based on the macro level constraints and the micro level priorities felt and expressed at the grassroot level. The relevant question that needs to be explored in this context is the replicability of these experiments. In other words, it is necessary to find out as to why the watershed development programme has remained isolated as a few examples and has not yet spread as a movement? There is an urgent need for a lot more studies at the grassroot level evaluating the performance of these programmes which will throw considerable light on the changing socio-political-economic structure at the micro level and its linkages at the macro level.

IV

The conclusions that emerge from the above discussion may be noted here briefly. The trends in the development thinking indicate, that the development theory is on the decline. However, the problem of underdevelopment has persisted in developing economies. In case of Indian economy too it has been observed that the development strategy implemented so far has failed to provide livelihood opportunities to the majority sections of the population. There is a growing need for the search of a new alternative strategy which will be both equitable and sustainable. Various experiments in watershed development programmes in the country provide such an alternative. Although they are still not widespread phenomenon, it is hoped that they have a tremendous potential to bring about the transformation of rural economy.

REFERENCES

Bharadwaj, K. (1990): Paradigms in Development Theory—Plea for 'Labourist' Approach, *EPW*, Vol, 25, No. 4.

Damodaran, A. (1991): "Tragedy of the Commons and Commedy of Common Property Resources", *EPW*, Vol. 26, No. 38.

Datye, K.R., Joy, K.J. & Patankar, B.: Development of Village Ecosystems—An Approach based on Equity, Productivity and Sustainability (Unpublished).

Datye, K.R. & Paranjape, S. (1990): Sustainable Agriculture in Semi-Arid Regions: Opportunities for Small and Marginal Farmers', *Wasteland News* (SPWD), Aug-Oct.

Ghosh, A. (1993): An Agenda for the South, *EPW*, Vol. 28, No. 16.

Govt, of India: Various Five Year Plan Documents.

Hussain, A. (1990): Resource Base Erosion and Sustainable Development in South Asia, EPW, Vol. 25, No. 33.

Jodha, N.S. (1990): Rural Common Property Resources—Contributions and Crisis, *EPW*, Vol. 25, No. 26.

Mundle, S. (1993): Policies, Paradigms and Development Debate at Close of Twentieth Century. *EPW*, Vol. 28, No. 36.

Sen, Pranab (1991): 'Growth Theories and Development Strategies'—Lessons from Indian Experience, *EPW*. Vol. 27, No. 30.

Vyasulu, V. & Others (1991): Towards A Political Economy of the Economic Policy Changes, *EPW*, Vol. 27, No. 38.

World Bank (1990): World Development Report.

5

Population Growth, Sustainable Development and a Threat to Environment

Dhirendra Nath Konar

Rapid growth of population all over the world, specially in the Third World countries, after 1950 has posed serious problems. Non-adherence to the Malthusian warning had brought catastrophe in our civilisation. A natural consequence of the high growth rate of population has been rapid urbanization and a relative negligence of the rural areas. But poverty in both the urban and the rural areas has been increasing. Finding no alternative, people have been exploiting nature in every possible manner. The nature, in her turn, has been taking the revenge in one form or another. Consequently, increasing degradation of the environment has been brought to light and a peaceful living in this beautiful earth has been at stake. The rate of growth of population is to be brought to around one per cent per annum in order that we may lead a comfortable life in the midst of our surroundings.

1. Population Growth Across the World

According to the Holy Bible the first man of this universe is Adam and the first woman is Eve, Adam's wife. Thereafter population of this world has been increasing in the natural way. From various sources it has been known that the population of this world was only 10 crores in 3000 B.C. At 1000 A.D. this population stood at 30 crores. The population of this world in different years has been presented in the following table.

World Population (crores)

Years	1650	1850	1900	1930	1960	1991	2001
Population	50	100	150	200	300	538	620 (estimated)

The content of the above table is self-explanatory. There can be no denying the fact that the world population has been increasing at a rapid rate, specially since 1950. It has been estimated that by 2001 the world population is going to be 620 crores.

However, it is true that the growth of population across the world is not of the uniform nature. This growth is really very surprising in the third world countries which are more or less caught in the second stage of the "theory of demographic transition" and in these countries the rate of growth of population is around 3 per cent per annum. The growth rate of population in the advanced countries which have attained the third stage of the above theory is about 1 per cent per annum. At present China is the most populated country of the world while India with only 2.4 per cent of the global land has been fostering about 15 per cent of the world population. From the standpoint of the birth rate alone, India has topped the list of the countries facing population problem. The annual incremental population of India is more than the total population of the entire continent of Australia. According to the 1991 census, we have about 87 crores of people. If the present trend of the growth rate of population in India continues, then by 2001 we will have about 100 crores of people and it will be a stupendous job to cope with such a big number of people.

2. Nature in the Rescue of Human Being

A study of the history of the development of human being will reveal that initially man had to be satisfied with the collection of food from nature herself. In the early days man had freely gathered vegetables, fruits and seeds from the plants and trees and had eaten raw meat of wild animals. In course of time the intelligent man, the most important creation of God, learnt the art of cultivation and in this field nature showed abundant bountiness. Then with the progress and development of agriculture man learnt the technique of industrialisation. However, there is an unambiguous distinction between agriculture and industry. This distinction had been made prominent by Adam Smith (1723-1790), the father of modern economics, in his famous book "Wealth of Nations" where he said, "....in industry and commerce the forces of nature are never brought into play whereas in agriculture they always collaborate with each other." Smith added, "No equal quantity of productive labour employed in manufacture can ever occasion so great a reproduction. In them nature does nothing; man does all; and the reproduction must always be in proportion to the strength of the agents that occasion it"

(*Wealth of Nations, Book II; 344*). The sum and substance of what Smith suggested is that it is agriculture which creates maximum surplus. This point may be classified with the fact that the paddy seeds worth 5 kgs sown on a fertile land may yield output of paddy even to the extent of 5 quintals. Such huge surplus is never generated in industry. That the surplus can be created in agriculture was first made prominent by the leader of the physiocratic school in France, Dr. Francois Quesney (1694-1774). This is what he termed "produit net" (or, net product) in his Tableau Economique.

3. Industrialisation and the Exploitation of Nature

After the development of agriculture man through further research went on towards industrialisation and with it a novel way of maintaining life was discovered. Man's comfort increased, man's time and energy were saved. But we have already seen that in industry the surplus created is relatively low. So man, in search of reaping more profit, started exploiting nature with a great blow. Man has mercilessly been cutting trees of the forest and he has been killing wild animals for getting their flesh, skins, bones and other valuables. Besides, many people with the passage of time have changed their food habit—they have become non-vegetarians. Naturally, for man's necessity many birds and innumerable animals are being killed day after day. The effect of all these unkind activities has been very dangerous—the ecological balance has been in danger. As a consequence, the nature has been expressing her wrath through drought, flood, earthquake and similar other disasters.

Moreover, the industrialists, in order to gain more profit and at the same time to reduce cost of production have been dumping huge wastes of the firm products in the nearby forest, river bed and sea shore. These things are being done with nominal expenditure and naturally that leads to a reduction in private cost. But that is very much adding to social cost. The environment is getting polluted—there is air pollution, water pollution and the like. Man's tension is increasing, there is breathing trouble, there is ear trouble and so on. Thus people fail to lead a peaceful and tranquil life—there is no peace at the place of work nor at the place of residence. We have been maintaining a higher standard of living but only at the cost of a sound physique and a peaceful mind. We have been sacrificing the avowed principle of maintaining a "good life" as propounded by the Greek economists of the ancient period.

With the growth of industrialisation there has now been a continuous spree for urbanization to which we now turn.

4. Growing Urbanization Across the World

Urbanization is a consequence as well as a causal factor in economic development. Obviously the rate of urban growth is an important index of the progress of an economy. There may be a number of factors leading to an increase of urbanization. These factors are: (*a*) the natural growth of the urban population, (*b*) migration from rural to urban areas and (*c*) the areas previously designed as rural areas passed into the urban category by satisfying some criteria. Of all these factors migration from rural to urban areas has become very significant now-a-days all over the world, specially in the developing countries. Behind this migration also lie a number of important factors, namely social, physical demographic, cultural and communication. It has been reported that more than 1,50,000 people are being added to urban population in the developing countries everyday. It has also been reported that the size of cities of these countries by the year 2000 is expected to double compared to 1980. With the growth of urbanization poverty in urban areas has also been increasing. In Latin American countries, for example, the number of urban poor increased from 44 million in 1970 to 115 million in 1990. Another feature of urbanization has been that urban population is getting concentrated principally in class 1 towns with a population of one lakh and above. It has been known that by 2015 the world will have 33 megacities with population of more than eight million and more than 500 cities with population of over one million. In India between 1951 and 1991 the rate of growth of urban population had been 3.7 per cent per annum and in the same period the rate of growth of people living in class 1 cities has been 5.1 per cent annum! It is surprising to note that of the twelve highly populated cities of the world Greater Mumbai and Greater Calcutta with a population of 12.6 million and 10.9 million respectively had occupied the sixth and the tenth places respectively in 1991. According to the World Health Organisation the ideal density of population per kilometre is 2500. But the figure for Calcutta is 32000 and that for Greater Mumbai is 13,671—this is simply unimaginable.

Another feature of urbanization is the ever growing population in the slums and shanty towns of the developing countries. Todaro in his *Economic Development in the Third World* states, "From the favellas of Rio de Janeiro and the pueblos or jovenis of Lima to the bustees of Calcutta and the bidonvilles of Dakar, such makeshift communities have been doubling in size every 5-10 years. Today slum settlements represent over one-third of the urban population in all developing countries; in many cases they account for more than 60 per cent of the urban total" (*p. 250*).

This unprecedented growth of urbanization will naturally exert stress on local environment and threaten the quality of life.

5. Population Pressure and Sustainable Development

A growing population needs a growing supply of food which is provided basically by the "Mother Earth". Naturally, there is always a race between rising numbers of people in the Third World countries and total food supplies. This race was predicted by Thomas Robert Malthus (1766-1834) in 1798 in his *Essay on the Principle of Population*. In course of time new breakthroughs in the technology of food production, commonly known as Green Revolution enabled many Third World countries to cope with the problem of food. But since 1970 it has been noticed that in addition to the growth of the Third World population, rising affluence in the developed countries has become a major factor in the annual increase in food demands. It is a fact that population growth remains the dominant source of expanding food demands. But rising income levels also account for an ever increasing proportion of this demand. This may be explained with an example. Across the World people in the less developed countries consume approximately 181 kg. per person per year and almost whole of this amount is consumed directly as bread and rice to meet minimum energy requirements. But an average North American consumes over 450 kg. per year, out of which only 65 kg is consumed directly in the form of bread and breakfast cereals while the remaining 385 kg per capita is consumed indirectly in the form of meat, milk and eggs. This means that 385 kg. of cereal grains per capita are used to feed livestock and poultry. How alarming this situation is! Will our "dear Mother Earth" be able to sustain this requirement for her sons and daughters? There is doubt over it.

There are four critical factors of modern agricultural production which have been putting serious resource constraints on its expansion. These are land, water, energy and fertilizer. The world food supplies may be expanded by two ways, namely (*a*) increasing the total amount of land under cultivation and (*b*) raising the productivity on existing arable land through the more intensive use of water, energy and fertilizer. But any attempt to increase productivity of land by these two means is constrained by the following factors.

Enlarging the area under cultivation has been the traditional approach for the expansion of agricultural production. But the possibility of further expansion of farm areas is limited now-a-days by the growing competition for land use by urbanization, industrial development and transportation.

Water so long learnt by the students of economics as a "free" good has now become scarce and naturally a critical input. In many parts of the globe people have been facing the problem of drinking water.

An alternative means of intensifying agricultural production on existing land is the application of greater energy inputs through the use of mechanized farm equipment. But the sharp increases in world oil prices make such efforts extremely costly.

Finally, supplies of fertilizers are now becoming more costly because of substantially higher prices for phosphate and potash and alternative uses for the petroleum into fertilizer production.

6. Conclusion and Suggested Policies

The pressure of population especially in many of the Third World countries, has enhanced the demand for food, drinking water and energy. At the same time the ever growing purchasing power of the affluent citizens of the world has intensified the demand for all these materials. The resultant of these two growing pressures has been such an increasing demand for food that it cannot simply be met up. The hungry man, in order to sustain the supply of food from the "Mother Earth" has been exploiting her, in every possible manner only to earn her wrath, curse and displeasure. It is high time that we, the people all over the world, realize this and apply common-sense and do the needful to make this beautiful world an abode for residing with the surroundings all around us in peace and tranquillity. To achieve this the following strategies may be recommended at the initial stage:

(*a*) The rate of growth of population should be checked to the maximum possible extent. The present annual growth rate of population of around 3 per cent should be reduced to around 1 per cent. For this education should be spread at all levels and women are to be involved in every possible manner. We should give more emphasis upon the dissemination of education, not of literacy.

(*b*) People should be made aware of the environment. To make this effective, study of environment should be made a compulsory subject in the school education. Besides, the "World Environment Day", the 5th day of June every year, should be celebrated in such a manner that people of all walks of life, specially the children and the younger ones, realize it whole-heartedly.

(*c*) The environment damaging activities should be forbidden by all means and for this strict vigilance should be kept throughout the year. At the same time environment fostering activities should be duly rewarded.

(*d*) There should be a limit to the running of vehicles along the streets and roads of the towns. The purchase of cars and other vehicles should be on the basis of urgency of necessity, not on the basis of ability to afford them.

(*e*) The relatively small towns should be endowed with new industrial centres and be provided with the basic amenities of life.

(*f*) The living conditions of villages should be improved. More and more emphasis should be put on the development of agriculture, rural industry and rural development.

REFERENCES

Bose, A (1974): *Studies on India's Urbanization 1901-1971*, Tata Mc-Graw Hill Publishing Company Ltd., New Delhi.

Konar, D.N. (1991): "Degree of Urbanization in Orissa and Bihar—An Econometric Analysis", *Arthashastra*, Vol. 10, Nos. 1 and 2, Calcutta.

_____ (1996): "Urbanization in West Bengal and the Problem of Environment", *Economic Affairs*, Vol. 41, Qr. 1, January-March, Calcutta.

Schumpetor, Joseph: *History of Economic Analysis.*

Smith, A.: *Wealth of Nations*, Vol. 1 and Vol. II.

The Statesman, May 6, 1996, Calcutta.

Todaro, M. (1987): *Economic Development in the Third World*, Orient Longman.

World Development Report, Various Issues.

World Resources Report, 1996-97.

6

Sustainability of Development and Economics of Environment in the Context of SAARC Countries

D.D. Guru

Among the various aspects of the literature on development the question of its sustainability has become a matter of greatest concern in the past few years on account of the environmental aspects of economics of development. The paper analyses the economics of environment in the context of SAARC countries. It starts with the examination of the economics of environment in the historical perspective. It deals more specifically the issue of exhaustible resources, the problem of 'externalities' and the concept of 'public good' in relation to the environmental degradation and depletion of resources. It then examines the different dimensions of environmental problems relating to (*a*) forest and deforestation, (*b*) water resources, (*c*) land and soil resource, (*d*) fertiliser and pesticides, (*e*) urban congestion, industrialisation and pollution, (*f*) marine and coastal resource degradation, (*g*) waste disposal, (*h*) acid rain and rising sea level in the context of SAARC countries. The paper argues for the necessity of making clearcut provisions for dealing with these environmental problems and hence with the issues of sustainability of development in SAARC framework in the form of creation of joint fund and modalities for assuring appropriate design of investment for providing sustainable development in terms of optimum use of environment bases from long-term point of view in the SAARC region.

Economics of Environment: An Overview

The environment has been a topic of intense concern, research and writings over the past few decades. Environment is a long-large word meaning all those outward things that surround us in our daily life. The environment is concerned with the relationship between the living organism and the natural factors influencing survival and the growth of the living organism. The life support system on this planet consists of air, water, land, flora and fauna. Normally these are mutually interconnected and also interdependent. The activities of man constitute one single factor which often disrupts the intricate balance among the constitutents of the life support system. In his eagerness to urbanise and industrialise, man has not only destroyed plant cover built up meticulously by nature over millions of years, but also polluted air, water and land so much so that development has become partly synonymous with deforestation and desertification and progress with pollution.

Environmental pollution has existed for many years in one form or another. It is an old phenomenon and yet in its contemporary forms it seems to have crept up on government and even on pertinent professional disciplines such as biology, chemistry, most of engineering and, of course, economics[1], and other social sciences.

Environmental economics is a new field, essentially the creation of the present generation of economists. But its roots are in the externalities theories of Marshall[2] and Pigou[3], the public goods theory of Wicksell[4] and Bowen, the general equilibrium theory of Walras[5] and the applied field of benefit-cost theory analysis foreshadowed by Dupuit[6] but cultivated to maturity by economists in the Water Resource Agencies of the U.S. Government. External effects of economic transactions have been recognised by economists for a long time. The 1920s saw a series of articles in Economic Journal dealing with possible external economies that were associated with investment in decreasing cost industries. But in addition, economic theory has long recognised the existence of "common property"[7] problems and resource misallocation associated with them.

The concern about the environmental degradation is on sharp increase. There are environmental trends that threaten to radically alter the planet, that threatens the lives of many species including human species. Each year 6 million hectares of productive dry land turns into worthless desert. Over three decades it would amount to an area roughly as large as Saudi Arabia. More than 11 million hectares of forests are destroyed yearly and this over three decades would equal an area about the size of India. There are other examples of environmental degradation.[8] The important factors responsible for the depletion and degradation of environment are, in one way or the other, related to the process of economic development and growth being pursued by the different countries. But the crucial question in this regard is whether there is the possibility of new era of economic growth based on policies that sustain and expand the environmental resource base.[9] This, naturally, raises the question of economic use of environmental resource base.

One of the important aspects of environmental economics deals with the problem of proper resource use. The resources are broadly classified into two categories *i.e.*, renewable and non-renewable. While the problem of sustaining the base of renewable resources is related to the question of the rate of use and the rate of replenishment, the problem becomes more complicated with regard to the use of non-renewable or exhaustible resources. On the basis of the Malthusian notion of fully exploiting the finite acreage of arable land, there developed the concept of land rent. In the twentieth century L.C. Gray[10] applied the concept of land rent in the context of exhaustible resource like coal. Later on this aspect of the extraction of exhaustible resources was dealt more fully in the use of appropriate mathematical method by Hotelling[11] known as Hotelling Rule. The Hotelling Rule maintained that marginal ton, extracted in any period should yield the same rent in present value terms. Jevons[12] (*1865*) foresaw a day at which the coal stock beneath Britain's soil would become exhausted. He, no doubt, entertained the idea that technical progress might delay the date of exhaustion but was pessimistic about disaster being delayed in the long run. He referred to coal as 'depleting capital good' and had suggested using revenues obtained from taxing coal sales to pay off the national debt. About hundred years after Jevons, Forrester[13] (*1970*) and Meadow's *et al.*[14] (*1972*) restated the general Malthusian position in simultaneous equation dynamic system. Attempts have been made through the use of computer-based models to predict how various economies in the world will react to the constraint of growth. Solow[15] (*1974*) developed formally the idea of new investment being a substitute for a currently partly depleted stock such as coal. Hortwick[16] indicated that the paths of constant consumption with stationary population could be sustained if current investment equalled current value of current depletion of finite homogenous stocks of exhaustible resources. In the case of copper, Nordhaus[17] (*1973*) made his view of exhaustibility popular through an empirical study of world energy production and consumption and suggested recycling as an imperfect means of renewing stocks for forestalling the disappearance of copper.

Externalities constitute another important aspect of environmental economics. In economic context an externality is said to exist when one firm's (or an individual's consumption) production affects the production process (or standard of living) of another firm (or individual) in the absence of market transaction between them.[18] The alternative terms for externalities are spillovers, external effects, or social effects. While the literature distinguishes between many kinds of externalities, one important classification having economic bearing is in terms of technological (non-pecuniary) and pecuniary externalities. While the pecuniary externality is concerned with individual decisions effecting change in price, the non-pecuniary externalities refer to more or less direct effects other than price changes that one decision unit might impose on another. Technological externalities can and in many instances do prevent market mechanism from functioning efficiently.[19] The theory of technological externality is the foundation of environmental economics.

In the context of environmental economics, the most important cause of market failure is the divergence between producer's evaluation of cost of his activities and the valuation by the society as a whole. This divergence arises because of the presence of externalities or spillover.

When a factory discharges its waste into river, the private cost to the factory of using river as a waste disposal system is zero. But the resulting pollution may require a downstream industrial user to purify the water before he can use it for industrial processes and he has to incur costs.[20] The contamination of water may kill fish stock and or make the water injurious for the health of the people. All these, naturally, entail social cost.

Following the pioneering work by Sidgwick[21] (*1887*) and Marshall (*1890*), Pigou (*1920*) had provided the basic theoiy of static technological externalities. Coase[22] (*1960*) has explained how initial rights could be assigned in various ways. Arrow[23] (*1969*) has explained how externalities could be internalised by creation of additional market. Buchanan[24] (*1969*) has studied second best problems associated with externalities. Starrett[25] (*1972*) has pointed out the associated problem of non-convexity.

Environmental pollution is a good example of negative externalities. There are three important functions performed by environment that has relevance for an examination of the concept of pollution as an externality. These are (i) environment acting as supplier of "natural goods", (ii) environment acting as supplier of natural resources which are used to create economic goods, and (iii) environment acting as a 'sink' into which the inevitable byproducts of production and consumption activities can be discarded. The last is known as the waste assimilative function of the environment. These three functions help to analyse the welfare economic foundations of environmental economics. In other words, these functions help us to analyse the externality implications of pollution that leads to market failure.[26] The natural goods provided by the environment and the environment's function as a waste assimilator have no market price.

If these services of environment were priced then the resulting pattern of use will be different from what it is when they are available as free goods or services. This treatment of environmental services and function as free goods result in market failure leading to non-optimal pricing. The environmental problems may thus be considered as problems of non-optimal pricing which is the core subject matter of welfare economics. Environmental economics can be considered to be a branch of welfare economics. Welfare economics attempts to assess what an optimal configuration of the economy is, what factors cause deviations from such optimality and how to correct such deviations. Environmental pollution is one of the important causes of deviation from optimality by creating divergence between private cost and social cost.[27]

Environment quality becomes a type of economic good and has its adverse impact on health. The problem of generation of pollution could be looked in the context of material balance approach of the economy which conceives the economic process as a physically balanced flow between inputs and outputs. If we begin with some given level of organic and inorganic inputs from the resource base of the economy, final goods are produced from these organic and inorganic inputs through various energy conversions and productive process during which waste residuals are generated and discharged into the environment. Such wastes are generated both from the production and consumption process. Economic growth cannot occur without additional extraction of resources from the environment and increased waste. The second Law of Thermodynamics depicts this process of material and energy transformation as an irreversible transformation of useful materials and energy into disordered, dissipated and useless waste. This law uses the concept of entropy which is a thermodynamic measure of amount of energy unavailable for useful work in a system undergoing change. Entropy is also considered as a measure of the degree of disorder in a substance or system; such that entropy always increases and available energy diminishes in a close system as Universe. Thus all environmental degradation can be defined as increased environmental entropy.[28]

The environmental problems are related to the concept of 'public goods'. Historically air, water and other natural resources have not been privately owned. This is because it is difficult and in most cases impossible to exclude people from the use of these resources. Non-excludability thus becomes an important feature of public good. The other equally important feature is non-rivalry in its consumption. It is these two features of public good which leads to their over-use, misuse and abuse. Individuals are induced to use environmental resources liberally which leads to creation of environmental problems. There is normally no tendency to protection of such resources. The protection of such resources is only possible through collective decision and action.

Environment and SAARC Nations

It will be interesting to examine the issues of economics of environment in the context of environment problems of the South Asian countries. We can take up the issue of collective action relating to environmental protection among the SAARC nations. The idea of regional co-operation in South Asia is not new. Countries of this region have co-operated with one another both bilaterally and regionally under the umbrella of such forum as ESCAP, the Non-aligned Movement and Commonwealth. These efforts have not fully exploited the vast potential of regional co-operation that exists and the consequential benefits that this will bring collectively and individually to the countries of the region. The feasibility of such co-operation had been discussed informally in various capitals of South Asian countries. But it was during late 1970s that the then President of Bangladesh Mr. Zia-ur-Rahman took initiative in the formation of some organisation of co-operation among the countries of the South Asia. He addressed a letter in this connection to the heads of the governments of countries of South Asia *viz.* India, Pakistan, Bhutan, Sri Lanka, Nepal, Maldives in which he proposed that countries of the region should explore the possibility of establishing some institutional arrangements for regional co-operation and pleaded for meeting at the summit level. The letter had good response from the governments. Meetings at the level of secretaries and ministers were held between November 1980 and December 1985. The fourth meeting of ministers of the participating countries was held at Dakka on 5th December, 1985 in which foreign ministries of the seven countries considered the text of the draft declaration submitted by the standing committee and recommended for its adoption by the summit. The charter of the South Asian Association for Regional Co-operation (SAARC) was approved by the Heads of the State or Government of all these countries at Dakka, Bangladesh on 8th December, 1985. It would be interesting to present some of the basic facts about the countries under the SAARC during its formation. The following table gives the details:

TABLE 1
SAARC Member Countries: Basic Facts during the Formation

Member Countries	Population 1983		GDP 1983 US $ million	GNP Per Capita 1983 US $	Share of Agriculture in GDP	
	in Millions	as percentage of the total			1960	1980
Bangladesh	101.5	10.17	10,640	135	9	38
Bhutan	1.4	0.14	113	96	5	3
India	762.2	76.38	16,870	193	50	31
Maldive	0.15	0.02	22	418	—	—
Nepal	17.8	1.70	2,180	145	67	61
Pakistan	99.2	9.94	25,800	360	46	26
Sri Lanka	16.4	1.64	4,770	340	32	21
Total	997.85	100.00	—	—	—	—

The table shows that countries of SAARC have large size of population but the size of per capita income is lower. The highest per capita income is found to be for Maidive at $ 418. Next comes Pakistan with $ 360. Sri Lanka's per capita income is at $ 340. Other countries have per capita income of less than $ 200. The economies of the region are mostly agricultural. There is the tendency of decline in thc share of agriculture in GDP. Nepal has the largest 61 per cent of GDP in agriculture.

In order to find out the nature of environmental problem facing the countries of the region it would be advisable to analyse the different types of environmental problems in the context of these countries. We propose to take up environmental issues under the heads of (1) Deforestation, (2) Water Resource Problems, (3) Land and Soil Resource Problems, (4) Fertilisers and Pesticides, (5) Urban Congestion, Industrialisation and Pollution, (6) Marine and Coastal Resource Degradation, (7) Waste Disposal, (8) Acid Rain, and (9) Rising Sea Level. These are generally the issues associated with environmental problems having significance to the countries of the region.

Deforestation: High population density has contributed not only to displacement of forest by land clearing for cultivation but also to deforestation from overharvesting of forest for fuelwood and fodder. India and Bhutan are the largest producers of fuelwood in per capita terms. Bhutan consumes approximately 1 cubic meter per capita per year compared to less than 0.25 cubic meter per capita by Bangladesh and Pakistan. There is large scale deforestation in India. The National Remote Sensing Agency of the Department of Space reports that area under more than 10 per cent tree cover decreased from 55.18 million hectares in 1972-75 to 46.08 million hectares in 1981-82. The depletion took place in regard to good forest with density of 30 per cent tree cover decreasing from 46.4 million hectares to 32.2 million hectares while the poor forest area between 10 per cent and 30 per cent increased from 8.75 million hectares to 10 million hectares.[29] The total area under forests in Bangladesh (1977) stood at 9283 sq. miles as compared to the geographical area of 55,598 sq. miles which comes to around 16 per cent of the geographical area. In case of Nepal not long ago 57 per cent of Nepal's land had forest cover. According to an estimate made by the State Planning Board Commission, the ratio has declined to 19 per cent. Taking South Asia as a whole forest area was reduced from 320 million hectares in 1850 to 175 million hectares in 1980 while crop land increased from 70 to over 200 million hectares in the same period.

Water Resources: The deforestation has direct impact on the water resources in the region. The felling of trees have interfered with the water cycle. Thus high rainfall in Cherapunji with its 12000 mm annual rainfall and its instant run off accentuates flood in Bangladesh and acute water scarcity in the most heavy rainfall area at the end of monsoon. Monsoon rainfall are neither evenly distributed as between different regions nor over time. In case of India for some regions the ground water withdrawals exceed recharge. This characteristic is present not only in Maharashtra and Deccan but according to Director General of ICAR, "at this rate of withdrawal of groundwater the foodgrain bowl of India, Punjab and Haryana could become waterless deserts in two decades". Floods are chronic problem in many of the SAARC nations. India and Bangladesh are the worst sufferers. River water disputes are common in the region. The rivers suffer from the problem of disposal of human sewerage and industrial wastes thereby affecting the quality of water of the rivers affecting the health of the people.

Land and Soil Resource Problems: Land is generally scarce in Asia and so also in the SAARC region. Soils are shallow, found in steeper slopes and face more drainage and tillage problems. Asian soil tends also to be chemically inferior to African and Central American soils. Because of high slopes, rapid rates of deforestation, poor drainage and inadequate soil conservation, soil in the region suffers from varying degrees of erosion, salinisation, waterlogging and desertification. In case of India 27 per cent land suffer from severe erosion. It is estimated that 80 million hectares in India and 14 million hectares in Nepal lose 6 billion tons and 0.24 billion of soil per year respectively.[30] Soil loss depends on many factors such as types of soil, slope, type and density of vegetation and rainfall intensity.

Fifteen per cent of land area in Sri Lanka, 24 per cent in Pakistan and 27 per cent in India are known to be affected by salinisation. Man induced salinisation and waterlogging results from poor irrigation practices, excessive irrigation and poor drainage which raise the water table and bring soluble salts to the soil surface. Studies have shown that by 1980, 130 million hectares of crop land in Asia was affected by waterlogging and salinisation, most of it being in China, India and Pakistan. Bangladesh suffers from saline water intrusion as far as 150 km in land owing to reduced water flows in the lower Ganges river. Moreover, 25000 sq. km of Bangladesh suffer from salinisation because of deteriorating water quality from tubewells because of overpumping.[31] Desertification is also an important environmental problem of the region. In arid and semi-arid areas and rangelands of South Asia particularly in India, Nepal and Pakistan desertification results from stocking range lands for in excess of their carrying capacity. Overgrazing results in patches of base soil which are vulnerable to erosion from heavy and infrequent rains. In drier areas exposed soils are also vulnerable to erosion by wind. Desertification also occurs in rainfed croplands as a result of inappropriate land use and fanning practices, excessive population pressure on land, cultivation of unsuitable land and inadequate investment in soil conservation.

Pesticides and Fertilisers: The uses of pesticides and chemical fertilisers have increased in the countries of the region on account of the adoption of high yield variety seeds and Green Revolution. Thus, the fertilizer consumption in India increased from 0.2 million tonnes in 1960 to 8 million tonnes in 1985 and the consumption of pesticides increased from 23 thousands tonnes to 91.2 thousands tonnes during the same period.[32] The uses of chemical fertilisers and pesticides have also increased in the other countries of the region. But it is being realised that long term use of chemical fertilisers and pesticides hamper soil regeneration without preventing crop pestidence.[33]

Urban Congestion, Industrialisation and Pollution: The general level of urbanisation is lower in the SAARC region but it is on increase. Pakistan has high urbanisation rate of around 32 per cent (1990) followed by India at 28 per cent and Sri Lanka at 21 per cent. Bangladesh at 14 per cent and Nepal at 10 per cent are at lower level. But the rate of growth in urban population in some of the important cities of the region is quite high and poses serious problems of pollution of various types. The increased urbanisation and industrialisation in the 1990s are likely to excerbate the already serious problems of crowding and water, air and noise pollution. The level of air pollution is mainly due to industrialisation and increasing use of automobiles. Congestion has caused increasing travel time for cars and public transport alike and air pollution, wear and tear of roads and lower quality of life for those living and working in heavily congested areas.

Industrial development and urbanisation are highly correlated. Industries in the developing Asian region of SAARC are often located at or near urban centres because of the distribution of public infrastructure. About half of the industrial value added in the countries of the region come from industries located in their largest urban centres. Correspondingly industrial pollution is concentrated in and around urban centres. It is often difficult to distinguish between observed environmental degradation caused by industrialisation and urbanisation. The absorption of large increase in labour force in the 1990s requires greater emphasis and attention on industrial development thus increasing the production and disposal of hazardous toxic chemicals and waste. This is already a major problem in India. In other countries of the region also the problem is assuming menacing proportions. Environmental pollution is a classic case of a public externality. It originates from variety of sources including discharge of domestic waste water, community solid wastes from agricultural activities such as excess pesticides and fertilisers The environmental pollution represents both a misuse of unpriced, open access resources and negative externality on sectors and individuals, who may not be parties to the pollution generating activity. This is because the environment serves both as recipient and residuals of economic activity and medium which transmits offsite effects to second and third parties.

Marine and Coastal Resource Degradation: Growing population and changing economic structure have affected the marine resources of the region. Rapid population growth and urbanisation, industrialisation and different forms of raw material extraction threaten the marine resource base of many countries of the region. With the exception of land locked countries of Bhutan and Nepal the rest of the countries of the region have large coastlines. Maidive and Sri Lanka have great dependence on the coastal and marine resources. A large proportion of population (more than 60 per cent) live in the coastal cities. Coastal and marine resources provide economic support for the population residing on the coastal areas as well as in the hinterland. The uncontrolled overuse and misuse of such coastal and marine resources leads to widespread degradation. The declaration of Exclusive Economic Zones (EEZ) by coastal states has brought into their jurisdiction resources which have previously been exploited by distant fishing nations. The degradation of coastal sea affects the health and income of the people.

Waste Disposal: The problem of waste disposal is growing on account of urbanisation and industrialisation. One of the important problems of waste disposal relates to the disposal of human sewerage. Domestic sewerage is a major source of degradation since municipal sewerage treatment systems are more the exception than the rule in the Asian countries in general and in the countries of the SAARC in particular. Thus only 4 per cent of India's population is served by sewerage system. Most of the municipal wastes generated by major cities in Pakistan such as Karachi, Rawalpindi, and Lahore ends up in the rivers that flow through these cities. Similar conditions prevail in other countries. Disposal of untreated sewerage in water bodies poses a threat to human health and acquatic life. As the biochemical oxygen demand for decomposition of waste rises with increasing loads of wastes from growing urban centres, dissolved oxygen will be eventually reduced to anaerobic level with consequent death of acquatic life. The problem of disposal of effluents by the industrial units brings about additional load on the assimilative capacity of water body thus hastening anaerobic conditions.

Acid Rain and Rising Sea level: While the problem of acid rain is not significant for this region, the rising sea level is certainly important for the two countries of this region. Maldive and Bangladesh are threatened by the rise in the sea level. The increase in sea level not only brings about the problem of floods but also poses serious threat to the low lying seashore areas of these countries. Bangladesh has witnessed serious flood situation in 1991 resulting in the death of around half a million population. Maldive had also serious floods recently.

The environmental problems presented above are just to indicate the areas in which joint efforts are desirable and required for providing proper solution to these problems. The problems indicated above could be tackled at individual country level also. But the better handling of these problems would be possible only if these are tackled at the regional level under the aegis of SAARC. This is because many of these problems are interlinked.

SAARC has been concerned with the problem of environment. In the initial stages of its formulation, environment including Marine Pollution Control was considered to be one of the 13 areas indicated for possible co-operation among these countries. Later on Kathmandu Declaration of November 4, 1987 specifically stated that: "The Heads of the state and government expressed their deep concern at the fast and continuing degradation of environment including extensive destruction of forest in the South Asian region. They also noted that South Asia was afflicted with such natural disaster as floods, droughts, landslides, cyclones, tidal waves which have particularly severe impact recently, causing immense human suffering. At the same time they expressed concern over the danger posed by global sea level rise and its effects on South Asian countries. These natural disasters and degradation of environment were severely undermining the development process and prospects of the member countries. They, therefore, decided to intensify regional co-operation with a view to strengthening their disaster management capabilities. They also decided to commission a study for the protection and preservation of the environment and to the causes and consequences of natural disasters in a well planned comprehensive framework."[34]

In the Fifth Meeting of the SAARC heads of the state and government held at Male from Nov 21-23, 1990, one of the important decisions taken was to designate 1992 as the SAARC Year of Environment.

The declarations and the resolutions about environmental protection, no doubt, have been made in the meetings of SAARC from time to time. No concrete steps have, however, been designed towards their implementation. Our discussion of the economics of environment in the earlier part has shown that the effective tackling of the problems of environment need to be taken in the form of associating appropriate investment plans for counteracting the evil effects of environmental degradation and their exhaustion keeping the long term view into consideration. As the problems of environment have also to take care of the problem of "externalities" it would be advisable that the externalities coming from the activities of the foreign countries are also taken proper care of. The negative impact of externalities could be neutralised in a better way if the actions are directed at the regional level than at the state level. It is, therefore, necessary that the problems of environmental control and the economics of environment in designing appropriate investment pattern for the control of environmental issues are handled at the SAARC level. This would lead to assuring a better resource base for dealing with development and environment balance in the countries of the region. Such an action should certainly not be a substitute for the actions taken at the different state levels but would be complementary to them. SAARC could think in terms of creation of a "*Joint Fund and Monitoring Arrangements*" for the proper direction of investment activities for safeguarding the environmental base for the region as a whole. The objectives and the modalities of its functioning could be a matter of details. The beginning however, could be made in placing this idea for consideration of the different member states and governments. This is necessary because SAARC functions on the basis of unanimity.

The working of SAARC is still in the formative process. Various types of suggestions are coming up for the proper orientation of the activities of SAARC.[35] The SAARC is the most populous regional grouping in the world. The countries of the region have large, rich and varied human and natural resources. The optimum utilisation of these resources from long-term point of view requires the intensification of co-operation among the member nations and also demands the proper consideration of economics of environment. The chances of arriving at agreement among nations of the region is immense. In any case it is worth quering it a trial.

REFERENCES

1. Kneese, A.V. (1992): Analysis of Environmental Pollution in Robert Dorfman and Nancy Dorfman (ed.) *Economics of the Environment*, W.W. Norton & Company, New York, p. 22.
2. Marshall, A.: *Principles of Economics*, 8th Edition, Book V. Macmillan & Co. London, pp. 378-80.
3. Pigou, A.C.: *Economics of Welfare*, 4th Edition, Chapter IX, pp. 172-203.
4. Wicksell, N. (1904): *Lectures on Political Economy*.
5. Walras, L. (1954): *Elements of Political Economy*. Allen & Unwin.
6. Dupuit, A.J. (1952): On the Measurement of the Utility of Public Works (Translated by R.H. Barbeck). *International Economic Papers*, No. 2. Macmillan, London.
7. Kneese, A. and Russel, C.S.: *Environmental Economics Encyclopaedia*, p. 159.
8. World Commission on Environment Development (1987): *Our Common Future* OUP, New Delhi p. 2.
9. *Ibid*., p. 3.
10. Gray, L.C.: Rent Under the Assumption of Exhaustibility, *Quarterly Journal of Economics*, Vol. 28, pp. 466-89.
11. Hotelling, H.: The Economics of Exhaustible Resources, *Journal of Political Economy*. Vol. 39, pp. 137-75.
12. Jevons, W.S. (1865): *The Coal Question: An Enquiry Covering the Progress of Nations and Probable Exhaustion of Coal Mines*, Augudus M. Kelley (Reprint). New York. 1915.
13. Forester, J.W. (1971): *World Dynamics*, Cambridge, Allen & Unwin Press.
14. Meadows, D.H., *et al.* (1972): *The Limits to Growth*, New York, Universe Book.
15. Solow, R.M. (1974): The Economics of Resources of Economists, *American Economic Review:* Papers and Proceedings, Vol. 64 (2) pp. 1-4.
16. Hortwick, J.M., *et al.* (1985): Preference for Output Price Uncertainty by Non-renewable Resource Extracting Term, *Economic Letters, Vol. 19 (1)*, pp. 85-90.

17. Nordhous, W. (1973): The Allocation of Energy Resources, *Brooking Papers on Economic Activity*, No. 3, pp. 529-70.
18. Karpagam, M. (1991): *Environmental Economics*, Sterling Publishers, New Delhi, p. 14.
19. Otto, A.D., *et al. Externalities, Information and Alternative Collective Action*, Dorfman & Dorfman (ed.) *op. cit.*, p. 73-74.
20. Binndha, V.D. (1991): Market System and Environment. Singh G., *et. al* (ed.): *Environmental Economics*, Mittal Publications, New Delhi, p. 44.
21. Sidgwick, H. (1887): *Principles of Political Economy*, 2nd Edition, London, Macmillan.
22. Coase, R.H. (1960): The Problem of Social Cost, *Journal of Law and Economics*, Vol. 3, pp. 1-44.
23. Arrow, K. (1969): The Organisation of Economic Activity: Issues pertinent to the choice of market *versus* non-market allocations. *An Analysis and Evaluation of Public Enterprises*. The PPB System, Washington DC, Government Printing Office, pp. 47-64.
24. Buchanan, J.M. (1969): External Diseconomies Corrective Taxes and Market Structure. *American Economic Review*, Vol. 50, pp. 174-6.
25. Starrett, D. (1972): Fundamental Non-convexities in Theory of Externalities, *Journal of Economic Theory*, Vol. 4, pp. 180-89.
26. Karpagam, M.L, *op. cit.*, p. 15.
27. *Ibid.*, p. 16.
28. Barbier, F.B. (1989): *Economics, Natural Resources Scarcity and Development*, Earthscan Publications, London, pp. 52-55.
29. Adiseshiah, M.S. (1989): Plan to Preserve Environment, *Yojna*, Aug. 15.
30. Asian Development Bank (1991): *Annual Report*.
31. *Ibid.*
32. *The Hindu* (1991): Survey of the Environment 1991, Madras, p. 119.
33. McDermott (1991): A Commitment to Land, *Span*, Vol. XXXII, No. 5, May, p. 3.
34. SAARC (1988): *From SAARC to SAARC* (1980-88), Kathmandu.
35. Dubey, M. (1991): Coping with Changing Realities of Global Economics, *Indian Express*, July.

7

Environmental Issues for Attaining Sustainable Development in LDCs

N. Manonmoney

In many Third World countries in the past, people had been keen about natural resources and the basic philosophy has been of harmony with 'Nature'. But to-day, the development activities of these countries are conflicting with 'Nature'. The environmental problems of several Third World countries are becoming acute and they need immediate attention in terms of investment, planning and expertise. In these countries, there are problems of mass poverty and rapid growth of population. There, the environmental problem is mainly related to resource depletion and resource conservation. In many Third World countries, depletion of renewable resources are at a faster rate than their regeneration. Therefore, in these countries, it is necessary to frame various economic activities that would pave way for the attainment of both sound environment and sustainable development. Sustainable development cannot be secured unless development policies pay attention for the accessibility of resources between generations. Therefore, the problem to-day is that of designing the development activities which have to offer the guarantee that the natural environment will persist. Today the issue is how should Third World countries treat natural environment in order that they can play their part in sustaining the economy as a source of improved standard of living.

The main theme of this paper is to discuss the need and importance of concerning the 'environmental aspects' in the development policies of Third World countries for attaining sustainable development. Man and his environment are a series of inter-related systems—physical, ecological, social, economic and political. A change in one system affects all the others. Thus the ecological consequences of development have therefore to be considered by all countries, particularly Third World countries and there is an urgent need to include 'sustainability in development' as one of the basic objectives in their economic planning.

Introduction

Today, the concept of 'eco-development' as a strategic approach for sustaining development including maintenance of environmental quality also in the goals of development policies has been broadly accepted by many economists. Till 1960s, the success of an economy was measured by its rate of growth and its Gross National Product. In late 1960s, there arose a question regarding the increase in the welfare of the economy as the resultant consequence of increase in goods and services—since the preservation of favourable ecological conditions became a real problem. In the beginning of 1970s, it was postulated to adopt economic stagnation or slow growth as a cure for ecological deterioration. But experiences have shown that the trade-off between economic development (short-term) and ecological protection (long-term) have not been satisfactory. This has led to an urgent need to counteract the prevailing methods of resource utilisation and bringing to halt the ecological degradation in the form of deforestation, soil erosion, desert expansion, climatic change etc., which result from inappropriate industrial and agricultural techniques and from the struggle to raise short-term productivity for stemming population.[1]

In many Third World countries, in the past, people have been keen about the natural resources and the basic philosophy has been of harmony with 'nature'. But today, exploding population, accelerated resource exploitation and development based on careless application of technology are the main causes/symptoms for environmental degradation in these countries. In this situation, what will happen to these countries? The mass of people will consume all that is produced without any thought for tomorrow and it would certainly end up in 'environmental mess' making their lives nastier and shorter. For many people in Third World countries, the quality of environment is at best a secondary consideration and entertain a wrong notion that when they become rich like DCs, then they could consider the problems of ecological disasters and find feasible solutions.[2]

In most of the Third World countries, the depletion of renewable resources take place at a faster rate than their regeneration. In such countries, it is usually through overexploitation or misutilisation of natural resources that the production potential will increase resulting in environmental losses. Thus in these countries, the sustainability of development should take into consideration the ecological aspects and should on no account endanger the natural capital. Sustainability requires the assurance of equitable access to the limited resources and adoption of appropriate technology to enhance the efficiency of natural resources.

The main theme of this paper is to discuss the need and importance of considering the 'environmental aspects' in development policies of the

Third World countries for attaining sustainable development. For this purpose, the following issues are raised and discussed: (1) What are the reasons for not including the environmental aspects in the development activities in the past? In other words, about the conventional economic approach towards the relationship between economic growth and environment. (2) What is the significance of framing development policies with environmental priorities for the sustainability of development in the Third World countries? (3) Can economic development and environmental conservation be made compatible? (4) What are the environmental aspects to be included in the economic policy of the Third World countries for sustainable development?

Conventional Economic Views on 'Environment'

The outmoded definition of the subject matter of economics namely increasing the production of goods and services is the aim of economic action is still alive in the minds of many people. Adam Smith (*1776*) was interested in material marketable goods. The material goods are valued in accordance with the costs of production. In 19th century, the concept of wealth was replaced by that of welfare. That is, it is a psychical and subjective quantity (satisfaction of human wants). Next evolved the concept of 'value'. The subjective value is caused by the discrepancy between wants and means of satisfying them, that is, by 'scarcity'.[3] It is felt that growth of production will increase the welfare. In economic theory, production is regarded as only one of the means that can contribute to welfare. 'Environment' is considered as a 'free good' and they are not discussed much in many economic theories.

In 1930s, John Maynard Keynes pointed out that the successful achievement of sustained economic growth would solve the basic economic problem of man—'scarcity'[4]. In contrast to traditional economists' views that society must maximise the flow of current output, Kenneth Boulding (*1966*) argued that earth's environmental resources should be viewed as essential irreplaceable social capital and the main purpose of economic activity should be to conserve this stock of natural capital intact for future generations.[5]

Presently, the visible environmental impacts have made it clear that environment consists of scarce and exhaustible resources. Economics as the science of allocating scarce resources among competing ends has now stressed the importance of conserving natural resources. Hence, now the subject matter of economics relates not to optimise growth level but to achieve sustainable development—that is care to be taken to see that development that meets the needs of the present generation does not affect the ability of future generations to meet their own needs. The modern economists, therefore, have twin responsibilities: (*i*) to preserve the environment without serious degradation, and (*ii*) to take measures to protect the environment without adversely affecting the flow of goods and services in the economy. It should, however, be noted that even towards the end of 1960s, there was a sudden public interest on matters regarding 'environment' and was realised that the economic activities of man (production and consumption) makes the earth an unfit home for human beings. Recently, this has been felt intensively by all over the world and therefore "ecological ideal" has become the popular concern of mankind today.

Importance of Environmental Priorities for Sustainable Development

Many Third World countries have achieved their independence only in the past 45 years. Many of these economies still depend upon the exchange of natural resources for capital and manufactured goods. There is not only economic gap between DCs and LDCs but there is 'ecological gap' also. The oil price shock of 1970s had brought negative environmental effects to the oil importing Third World countries. The balance of payment crisis had also led to rapid depletion of natural resources to stabilise their balance of trade.[6]

Today, nearly 25,000 species of plants and above 1,000 of animals can be declared as those which are under threat of extinction. About two-thirds of all terrestrial species are found in Third World countries and about 40 per cent of all species are using tropical rain forests as their habitat. About 40 per cent of world medicines in use are derived mainly from natural products. The loss of species in the Third World countries affect the yield of some medicines and pharmaceutical industries in DCs.[7]

Many Third World countries have too little interest in the long-term protection of species as there is lack of economic incentives for it. Thus, the chain linking rational economic utilisation and guaranteed ecological endurance is broken due to limited influence of long-term thinking and the logic of day-to-day survival. In the Third World countries in the past, some resources have been considered to be plenty in supply but now all resources are considered to be limited in supply. Now the issue is how should these countries treat natural environments in order that they can play their part in sustaining the economy as a source of improved standard of living?

It is observed that the two functions of the natural environment—resource supplier and waste assimilator—implied certain rules of resource and environmental management to be observed. Maintaining the services and quality of the stock of resources over time is possible by accepting the following two rules:[8] (*i*) Utilise renewable resources at rates less than or equal to the natural rate at which they can generate—that is, the rate of use is not greater than the natural regeneration rate; and (*ii*) keep waste flows to the environment at or below the assimilative capacity of the environment. These two main economic functions namely, resource supply and waste assimilation can be regarded as components of one general function of natural environment. For the foreseeable future, environment has to survive and this environment is needed to fulfil human values. The problem today is that of designing economic policies in such a way that it guarantees the prevalence of natural environment persistently. It is very hard to frame tools and analysis which demonstrate whether any particular economy is consistent with the natural environment or not. But it is accepted that for 'sustaining' an economy, it becomes important to establish some conditions for the compatibility of economies and their environments.

In 1980s, the term sustainability has appeared more predominantly. A proper definition of sustainable development might be as follows: it involves maximising the net benefits of economic development subject to maintaining the services and quality of natural resources over time. Economic development relates not only to increase in real per capita income but also to other elements in social welfare.[9]

Invariably many Third World countries rely on natural resources far more directly than developed countries. Firewood is used for fuel; water is used without treatment; shelter requires wood; food supplies ultimately depending upon subsistence agriculture and soil fertility. The sustainability of these countries depend on the maintenance of stocks of these natural resources. But these countries do not achieve sustainability because the margin of flexibility is very low and the man-made capital is frequently inadequate. Thus, there is an urgent need to maintain natural capital for more resilience to shocks and to ensure sustainable economy.

One more reason for maintaining the resource stock is to ensure equal access to it by future generations. It is realised that the possibilities of increasing 'natural capital' are meagre and remote. In many cases, the environmental losses incurred are irreversible. If the environmental damages are not arrested immediately it is highly regretable that the future generation cannot secure access to the resources if it comes to the point of extinction.

In many Third World countries, the efficiency gains got through economic activities will be quickly absorbed by rapidly increasing population. Thus, the rules of environmental management have to be designed to imply that the stock of renewable resources and the amount of waste assimilative capacity should not decline. For ensuring sustainable development the rate of utilisation of renewable resources has to be within the limits of regeneration. The uses of non-renewable resources have to be reduced and the stocks have to be available for future generation. Does this mean that these resources should not be used by the present generation? No. Not at all! While the development policies are aiming at using these non-renewable resources—the availability of their stocks is to be taken into consideration. Proper technologies should be adopted to economise the use of these resources.

The sustainable development requires the regulation of the mode of investment so as to minimise the negative impacts on air, water and other natural resources and to enhance both current and future production potential to meet the needs of people in the Third World countries.

Here one may raise the question as to whether it is possible to keep the stocks of natural resources constant in physical terms in real practice? In Third World countries, the basic needs of large number of people such as food, clothing, shelter and employment are not met. But sustainable development is possible only when the basic needs of people are met by increasing the productivity of the economy and by ensuring equitable opportunities for all. Thus, these countries have to manage natural resources so as to improve the sustained yield and waste assimilative capacity: river flow can be augmented, forests can be managed to improve timber yield, pasture and grazing land can be fertilised and seeded and so on.[10]

Economic Development *versus* Environmental Conservation

There has always existed trade-off between environmental quality and income growth. More particularly in the Third World countries, there is a greatly pronounced conflict between the need to increase incomes and the need to conserve natural resources. Further if these countries look into the future, there will be closer link between environment and development. Actually the conflict between economy and ecology can be attributed to two incompatible basic principles namely the ecological principle of *stability* and the economic principle of *growth*. The fear is that with the present situation of ecological depletion in what way these economic principles and policies be changed, reshaped and finally brought into harmony with ecological principles.

To bring harmony ecological accounting and the integration of environmental aspects into national accounting procedures are now developing. Under ecological accounting, there is the requirement that the physical quantity of natural capital stock would be valued in money terms and the economic approach has to aim at computing the overall aggregate money value—just like that of estimating national wealth. There is need to estimate implicit or shadow prices. No one has so far given a convincing assessment of natural capital stock and the significance of ecological losses and their long-term impact upon the economic earning power for growth.

Ecological accounting technique which not only may guide investment decision-making but also it will make the people to realise the economic significance of natural resources. If monetary value has been given for the stock of natural resources it will compel the people to economise the use of resources and it may act as a public information technique which in its turn can contribute to determine and promote qualitative economic processes. The monetary environmental reporting is needed by incorporating economic phenomena with environmental problems.

Environmentally-oriented Economic Policies and Sustainability of Development

It is not sensible to assume that environmental deterioration is an economic crisis peculiar to DCs alone. Pollution which was confined to DCs is increasingly being exported to the Third World countries also. Today, many multinational corporations locate their investments in high pollutive and high energy and natural resources consuming industries in these countries. Even though the ecological/environmental problems in the Third World countries are not as serious as in DCs, the poor countries are asked to take measures to protect their environment/natural resources and do not commit the same mistake in the name of economic development. At present many world organisations have realised that economic development cannot succeed unless development planning includes careful and sufficient attention to the natural environment. Short-term increase in food production through technological improvements cannot solve world hunger problems if they are achieved at the expense of the long-term productivity of the land. Conventional economic policy is based on the guiding principle of maximising flows: volume of production, income, profits—stated as "through-put economy" by Kenneth Boulding. But today there is need for "ecological economy"—that is increasing efficiency and maintaining resources. Thus, it aims at attaining environmental quality and resource conservation.

There seems the need to re-assess economic growth targets and to include "environmental stability" as one of the goals of economic policy of the Third World countries. Traditional taxes have to replace with emission charges and resource taxes. It is necessary to include environmental impact assessment in all economic decisions. The principle of responsibility and liability is to be re-established in these countries. Environmental legislations have to be strengthened and the polluting parties have to be made liable for compensation for the damaged parties. This principle will help to improve environmental quality through ecological self-regulation of business activities. It is needed to develop new technologies that incroporate ecological wisdom as well as scientific improvement. The cost of this new technological transformation may be high but for the survival of human community, this cost has to be met. The rates of resource depletion would be reduced by more efficient recycling methods and by using more pollution free power resources such as solar energy, wind energy, etc. That is, substitutability between exhaustible and renewable resources is needed. Moreover, to allow for the fact that a given standard of living can be secured from a reducing stock of resources, these Third World countries are needed to use less amount of energy to produce one unit of GNP than they did in the past.

Following two basic considerations need to be adopted to achieve sustainable development in the Third World countries:[11] (1) Development needs to be undertaken in relation to the qualities and limitations of the environment; and (2) Technological developments would be adopted with minimum environmental hazards. These considerations are needed in these countries for sustaining environment for future.

Ecological/environmental conservation is the very basis of all development as 'environment' is the most basic of all resources for development. In the Third World countries the development must be determined for ecologically sustainable, socially desirable and economically productive ways of using resources and these must be given concrete support in practice.[12] Bringing better harmony between economy and ecology is a difficult task both in theory as well as in practice. To enhance the quality of life of human beings in the Third World countries, it is necessary to re-orient the economic policy as "ecologically-oriented economic policy". Today, environmental aspects are to be included for maintaining sustainability of development. How to safeguard and enhance the environment for present and future has been the problem confined not only to the Third World countries but also for all countries of the world. Today, all nations in the whole world are moving towards a "common future" through environment on which the existence of the entire human community depends.

The author is grateful to Dr. (Mrs.) Savitri Arputhamoorthy, Reader in Economics, Madurai Kamraj University, for her valuable suggestions for writing this paper.

REFERENCES

1. Udo, Ernst Simonis (1984): Developing Countries in the Environmental Crisis, *Inter-Economics*, September-October, p. 239.
2. Seneca, Joseph J. and Taussig, Michael K. (1979): *Environmental Economics*, Englewood Cliffs, p. 360.
3. Hueting, Roefie and Leipert, Christian: Economic Growth, National Income and the Blocked Choices for the Environment, *WZB*, Berlin, pp. 2-3.
4. Keynes, John Maynard (1963): *Economic Possibilities for Our Grand Children*, New York: W.W. Norton & Company Inc.
5. Seneca, Joseph J. *op. cit.*, p. 352.
6. Udo, Ernst Simonis, *op. cit.*, pp. 239-240.
7. *Ibid.*
8. Pearce, David W. and Turner, P. Kerry (1990): *Economics of Natural Resources and the Environment*, Britain: BPC Wheatsons Ltd., p. 44.
9. *Ibid.*, pp. 46-48.
10. *Ibid.*, p. 50.
11. Mountjoy, Alan, B. (ed.) (1978): *The Third World Problems and Perspectives*, London: Macmillan Press Limited, pp. 19-21.
12. Udo, E. Simonis (1988): Ecology and Economic Policy, *Indian Journal of Environmental Health*, Vol. 30, No. 3, pp. 197-201.

8

Environmental Implications of Economic Development in an Input-Output Framework

Prakash and Sumitra Chowdhury

Socio-economic development hinges upon the rates and patterns of exploitation of resources, both human and material, and the technology in use. Industrialisation has, however, been the instrument of transformation of backward agrarian economies into developed ones. The ever urgent need for the raising and diversifying of standards of living of explosively growing population has warranted exponential increase in the exploitation of resources for production. Growth with equity, welfare and stability have also raised resource requirements. The rising level of exploitation and almost indiscriminate use of resources, especially the natural ones, have often led to the environmental degeneration. Explosively growing population and rapid economic development have exercised intense pressure on scarce natural resources, like land and forests.

Ecology has, however, been treated as exogenous to the socio-economic systems in conventional analysis. The complex inter-relations between different components of socio-economic systems warrant endogenisation of the so-called externalities such as economic system into the design of development in an integrated and inter-related framework of analysis. Input-output economics furnishes an appropriate instrument of analysis of an integrated system of this nature. But final demand and its growth are treated as exogenous in input-output models, whereas inter-relations between the growth of final demand, growth of output and its impact on eco-system in general, and forests, in particular, warrant the endogenisation of the growth of final demand on the one hand, and forests, on the other. In this paper, a segmented and sequential model of growth of consumption and output has been developed which is based on the synthesis of macro multiplier-acceleration processes of growth into a disaggregated inter-sectoral input-output model.

Introduction

Socio-economic development hinges upon the rates and patterns of exploitation of resources, both human and material, and the technology in use. Industrialisation has, however, been the instrument of transformation of backward agrarian economies into developed ones. The overurgent need for the raising and diversifying of standards of living of explosively growing population has warranted exponential increase in the exploitation of resources for production. Growth with equity, welfare and stability have also raised resource requirements. The rising level of exploitation and almost indiscriminate use of resources, especially the natural ones, have often led to the environmental degeneration. Explosively growing population and rapid economic development have exercised intense pressure on scarce natural resources, like land and forests.

Ecology has, however, been treated as exogenous to the socio-economic systems in conventional analysis. The complex inter-relations between different components of socio-economic systems warrant endogenisation of the so-called externalities such as economic system into the design of development in an integrated and inter-related framework of analysis. Input-Output economics furnishes an appropriate instrument of analysis of an integrated system of this nature. But final demand and its growth are treated as exogenous in input-output models, whereas inter-relations between the growth of final demand, growth of output and its impact on eco-system, in general, and forests, in particular, warrant the endogenisation of the growth of final demand on the one hand, and forests, on the other.

Multiplier-Accelerator Model

A segmented and sequential model of growth of consumption and output has been developed, which is based on the synthesis of macro multiplier-acceleration processes of growth into a disaggregated inter-sectoral input-output model.

Leontief static model may be taken as the starting point:

$$(I - A)X = F \quad (1)$$

where, X is gross output vector, F is final demand vector, A is input-output co-efficients matrix, and I is an identity matrix. Final demand consists of two components: consumption and investment—both public and private, where exports and imports may cater to both consumption and investment demand: $F = C + K$, where C and K are final consumption and investment sub-vectors of final demand. Solution value of X may then be split into two components: investment component and consumption component

$$X^1 = (I - A)^{-1} C \tag{2}$$

and $$X^2 = (I - A)^{-1} K; \tag{3}$$

value added component of X will, in fact, activate the inducement mechanism. Hence, the solution may be worked out in terms of value added vector V.

Growth of X, and hence, income, depends upon growth of K and its productivity. If, however, output/income grows, C will also grow, whereas, planned growth of output is designed to meet anticipated growth of demand for consumption. Multiplier-accelerator processes capture the essence of inter-related growth of investment, consumption and income. Incorporation of the twin processes sequentially will facilitate endogenisation of the growth of consumption demand in input-output framework, leading to the synthesization of Keynesian concepts into Leontief structure.

Disaggregative sectoral model envisages B = [B(j)]; B is a diagonal matrix of capital co-efficients where $B(j) = \sum_i b(ij)$, and b(ij) is the stock of *i*-th good per unit of output of good j. Keynesian multiplier-accelerator model may be formulated in Leontief framework:

$$Y = S^{-1} K = (I - C)^{-1} K$$
$$= (I + C + C^2 + C^3 + \dots\dots\dots + C^m)K \tag{4}$$

where S is the diagonal matrix of marginal propensities to save in commodity terms; C is the corresponding matrix of consumption propensities. Denoting successive rounds of accelerator-multiplier process by superscripts, the income/value-added, generated in the process of satisfying the investment component of final demand, will be

$$Y^0 = V(I - A)^{-1} K = V(I - A)^{-1} BGX \tag{5}$$

where $$K = B\Delta X—BGX$$

V is the diagonal matrix of value-added per unit of sectoral output; G = [g (i)] is the diagonal matrix of sectoral growth rates, and superscript 0 denotes initial period. The corresponding consumption levels will then be given by:

$$CY^0 = CV(I - A)^{-1} BGX \tag{6}$$

Income and consumption in the subsequent rounds will be given by

$$Y^1 = V(I - A)^{-1} CY^0$$
$$CY^1 = CV(I - A)^{-1} CY^0 \tag{7}$$
$$Y^2 = V(I - A)^{-1} CY^1 \tag{8}$$

... and so on.

If the initial consumption component of final demand vector is denoted by C, the ultimate final demand will be given by:

$$F = C + K + [I - CV(I - A)^{-1}]\ CV\ (I - A)^{-1}\ BGX$$
$$= C\ [I + \{I - CV\ (I - A)^{-1}\}^{-1}\ CV\ (I - A)^{-1}]\ BGX \qquad (9)$$

substituting for F from (9) into (1) we get

$$X = (1—A)^{-1}\ [C + \{I + [1—CV(1—A)^{-1}]\}^{-1}\ CV\ (1—A)^{-1}]\ BGX \qquad (10)$$

Implications of output vector X compatible with final demand vector F for deforestation may, then, be determined on the basis of the following model.

Model of Deforestation

Implications of output levels X^1 and X^2 as determined above for deforestation may be worked out. First money values of output are converted into physical quantities:

$$Q(i) = X(i) / \overline{\Pi}\ (i) = [1/ \overline{\Pi}\ (i)]\ \Sigma A\ (ij)\ F(j) \qquad (11)$$

where Q refers to the physical quantity, X is money value, $\overline{\Pi}$ is unit price, and A(ij)'s are the elements of Leontief inverse. Let i refer to wood, while the yield of wood per tree depends upon the age and variety of trees. The average yield of wood per tree of each variety may be used to estimate the number of trees to be felled to meet the requirements of wood:

$$T(i) = Q(i)/O(i) \qquad (12)$$

where T(i) denotes trees of i-th type and O is wood per tree. Total area to be deforested will then be given by

$$\sum_i E(i) = \sum_i [T(i)/N(i)] \qquad (13)$$

where E(i) is area and N(i) are trees of i-th type grown per square kilometer of area.

Final Demand and Output

Multiplier-accelerator model has been prognosticated with empirical data discussed in the appendix. Since the growth rates are proportionate, the model has been worked out iteratively for each successive year from 1979. Empirical results show that the model captures the real situation of 1979 very closely. The degree of closeness of estimated and actual sectoral output has been evaluated by MAPE (Mean Absolute Percentage Error) statistics. MAPE statistic has a value of about 9 per cent which is acceptable (*Prakash, 1989*). As expected the model furnishes overestimates of some sectors and underestimates of certain other. Hence, the degree of over and underestimation differs from sector to sector. Whereas, 15 out of 37 sectors are characterised by overestimation, the rest furnished underestimates of both final demand and gross output of the corresponding sectors. The simulation of the model can, however, reduce the estimation error to a great deal. Since, the degree and direction of backward and forward linkages differ from sector to sector, the rounds over which multiplier-accelerator process are spread also differ among sectors. The solution values of output and consumption have, however, emerged for every sector after the termination of maximum eight rounds. Consequently, multiplier-acceleration effect as measured by ultimate value of output differs significantly among different sectors. Interestingly, the number of rounds over which the multiplier-accelerator processes are spread, and their ultimate income effect, are directly related which is supported by the fact that coefficient of rank correlation between these two is as high as 0.85. It may, therefore, be hypothesised that the ultimate multiplier-acceleration impact of an initial change on different sectors will directly depend upon the dynamic sectoral linkages (*Prakash, 1986*).

Deforestation

The estimated sectoral final demand and output have then been used for estimating their implications for deforestation.

Division of the volumes of output, equalling the product of prices and quantities for three forestry sectors, that is, forestry and logging, wood and wood products, and furniture and fixtures converts monetary output into physical terms, whereas total wood requirements have been derived from equation (12).

Gross output levels for satisfying estimated levels of final demand in 1979 will require 105011947 cubic feet of wood and 30626 tons of forest materials like bamboo, cane and broomsticks as intermediate inputs. For producing the above quantity of wood 1141434 trees will have to be felled. The felling of trees will, however, have much more serious ecological implications than the uprooting of other forest materials like bamboos, cane and broomsticks. Thus, apart from the quantities involved, the changing structure of the output to be delivered by the forestry sector for meeting current and development needs of the economy will have differential bearing upon the ecology.

The area to be deforested for meeting these output requirements is approximately 17560.8 square kilometers in a period of only one year. In 1984-85 only 22.1 per cent of total geographical area of the country has forest cover which has been reduced to 21.9 per cent (667300 sq. km.) in 1986-87. If deforestation continues at this rate, the total forest cover available in 1986-87 will be eliminated in a period of only about 38 years if the remedial measures to control demand, on the one hand, and the programmes of reforestation and afforestation are not urgently taken up immediately.

The contentment of autonomously growing demand may need strong policy interventions both prohibitive and inducement based. The prices of forest produce relative to the prices of possible substitutes may have a direct bearing upon the bulging demand. But here also options will have to be exercised carefully. For example, substitution of wood and wood products by alluminium and steel products may have even more serious ecological implications than deforestation. Deep mining not only pushes non-renewable resources towards exhaustion but it may also inflict far more environmental damage than deforestation.

Conclusions

The main findings of the study are as follows:

(*i*) the prognostication of the multiplier-acceleration model establishes its empirical validity,

(*ii*) ultimate multiplier-acceleration effect differs among sectors,

(*iii*) the nature and strength of sectoral linkages have a direct bearing upon multiplier-acceleration effect,

(*iv*) the number of rounds over which the multiplier-acceleration processes are spread are directly inter-related which, in fact, reflects the sectoral linkage effect,

(*v*) the current levels and patterns of growth have serious implications for deforestation. Assuming that an annual rate of deforestation of 17560.8 sq. km. in 1978-79 to remain in operation, it will take about 38 years for completely denuding the entire forest cover of the country as per 667300 sq. km. in 1986-87,

(*vi*) policy interventions including appropriate pricing of forest produce may arrest the trend, but options are required to be carefully evaluated.

REFERENCES

Central Statistical Organisation, Dept, of Statistics, Ministry of Planning, Govt. of India: *Input-Output Transactions Table, 1978-79 and 1973-74.*

Chowdhury, Sumitra, (1987): *Levels and Patterns of Production of Forest-Based Industries and Their Impact Upon Ecological Balances in Meghalaya.* Unpublished M. Phil. Thesis, NEHU, Shillong.

Dutta Mazumdar, D.K., (1985): Capital Co-efficient Matrix for Indian Ecology. *Application of Input-Output Techniques to Growth and Trade*, Proceedings of 20th Anniversary International Conference of Input-Output Research Association, Part-II, NEHU. Shillong. Dec. 2-8.

Prakash, S., (1986): *Impact of Inventory Investment Upon Productive Capacity and Multiplier-Acceleration Process of Growth in Indian Economy*, Paper presented at International Workshop on Business Cycles Growth, August, Balatone.

— (1989): *Validating and Testing of Models of Education: Methodological Review.* Proceedings of National Workshop on (July 21-22), NIEPA, New Delhi.

Appendix

Data Base: The empirical prognostication of the model outlined in the text is based on input-output tables of the national economy for 1973-74 and 1978-79 prepared by Central Statistical Organisation. The base for capital co-efficient matrix is "*Capital Co-efficient Matrix for Indian Economy*" prepared by Dutta Mazumdar. However, A-matrices for both 1973-74 and 1978-79 consist of sixty sectors, whereas B-matrix consists of 33 sectors and is available for 1973-74 only. Hence, the first task has been to match the sectoral classification of A and B matrices. This leaves us with matrix A having 37 sectors of which five are service sectors. Sectors like defence about which information is scanty have been left out. Sectors like public administration having low capital base have also been left out. For the remaining service sectors, A matrix norm has been adopted for capital structure. For empirical prognostication of the model diagonal elements of matrices V, G and C have been compiled appropriately. Elements of C have been derived as the ratio of differences between final demand to gross output of 1978-79 and 1973-74. Cyclical fluctuations of output and final demand for sugar, cement, and storage and warehousing lead to negative marginal propensity to consume of these three commodities which is theoretically inadmissible. It is, therefore, assumed, that marginal and average propensities are equal in equilibrium On this assumption average of two average propensities to consume at two points of time has been taken as representing marginal propensities to consume for these commodities. Sectoral growth rates have been worked out on the basis of gross output/final demand from the two points in time.

TABLE 1:
Estimated Final Demand and Output for 1978-79 (in Rs. Lakhs)

Sl. No.	Sectors	Estimated Final Demand	Estimated Output	Ultimate Rounds of Solution
1.	Agriculture	3076310	4830663	7
2.	Forestry & logging	44639	70980	8
3.	Mining	19021	277682	6
4.	Sugar	75099	189415	4
5.	Food products excluding sugar	646170	802299	5
6.	Textiles	773265	998678	6
7.	Wood and wood products	11040	126832	5
8.	Furniture and fixtures	17712	20679	5
9.	Paper, printing and allied activities	45302	158295	5
10.	Leather and leather products	70785	89814	5
11.	Plastic and rubber products	9357	128409	5
12.	Petroleum products	55352	240704	5
13.	Chemical and chemical products	78807	690166	5
14.	Cement	351	46373	4
15.	Non-metallic products	93934	223916	6
16.	Iron and steel industries and foundries	26307	446860	7
17.	Other basic metal industries	8863	100352	5
18.	Metal products except machine and transport equipments	39708	119599	6
19.	Non-electrical machinery	28073	377144	5
20.	Electrical, electronic machine and equipments	51164	281006	5
21.	Railway transport equipments	702	83813	5
22.	Other transport equipments	66997	230766	5
23.	Miscellaneous manufacturing industries	153723	187205	6
24.	Construction	73542	1143410	5
25.	Electricity	41121	256834	6
26.	Gas and Water supply	12036	36249	5
27.	Railway transport services	104172	176447	6

(Contd...)

Sl. No.	Sectors	Estimated Final Demand	Estimated Output	Ultimate Rounds of Solution
28.	Other transport services	310251	700078	6
29.	Storage and warehousing	10	11519	5
30.	Communication	46953	84351	6
31.	Trade	782249	1643551	7
32.	Hotels and restaurants	269335	275313	4
33.	Banking	49703	239344	6
34.	Insurance	44381	65877	7
35.	Education and research	275736	275758	2
36.	Medical and health	116557	217306	3
37.	Other services	103083	381971	6

MAPE of estimated output = 0.093385.

9

Industrial Growth, Environment and Ecology in India: A Note

P.L. Sablok

Industrialisation is an economic process by which structural transformation of a subsistence economy is achieved. Industrialisation provides a wide range of consumer choice, increases productivity and standard of living, creates industrial skill, promotes innovation and technological development, promotes capital formation through higher wage incomes and diverts surplus farm labour to modern industry. To realise these benefits and hasten up required socio-economic changes, industrialisation is assigned top priority in underdeveloped countries like India.

Indian economy is an open, mixed and developing economy. Both public and private sector co-exist. They are actively engaged in enriching the GNP of the country. Development planning which has been adopted in India, has a fundamental means to transform the economy since 1951. Industrialisation is, however, considered to be the potent instrument for India's economic development and modernisation.

India, so far had implemented Seven Five Year Plans and three annual plans (1966-69) and now Eighth Plan has been implemented from 1st April, 1992. An overview of various Draft Five Year Plans set some much professed objectives of planning for industrialisation in India. They are rapid growth of output, employment, exports and import substitution, achieving balanced sectoral development, developing a balanced industrial structure having basic and heavy industries and balanced regional development, preventing the growth of exploitative monopolies, promoting a harmonious and complementary relationship between the public and the private sectors. These objectives have output, employment, income and spatial redistributive justice goal orientation.

In components of natural world, forest, air, water, soil, the sea and so on together make up the system called environment which supports all life in the earth planet. Environmental deterioration has taken place as a result of various kinds of exploitation of resources which has exceeded the safe limits. In recent years economists have devoted increasing attention to the interrelated problems of population, energy, pollution and resource depletion. Economics as a science of scarcity has much to say about these areas. Ecologists look at pollution in terms of the disruption of complex system of plant and animal life.

Environmental considerations should be integrated while encouraging industrial growth. The action points in this regard should include a mix of promotional and regulatory steps such as incentives for environmentally clean technologies, operationalisation of "polluter pays principle" by introducing effluent tax, fiscal incentives for pollution control, location of industries as per environmental guidelines, enforcement of pollution control norms and introduction of "Environmental Audit" etc.

Ever since the First Five Year Plan, India has been investing most of its resources and hopes on industry regarding it as the engine of growth. But analytical and insightful information available on Indian industry has remained in inverse proportion to the rising investments on this sector. The burden of the overview is that Indian planning and its industrialisation strategy suffered chronically from not only import substitution obsession but also from chronic export pessimism. Export pessimism, made the plans indifferent, if not opaque, to the potential of world demand and to the opportunity for using 'exports' as a dynamic instrument of India's industrialisation. The default by the planners, was all the more shocking since world demand was on the rise and expanding—implying that export pessimism was totally unwarranted.

Self-reliance has been a principal objective of Indian industrial planning although it is worth noting that the Second Five Year Plan (1956-61) made no mention of it. The concept of self-reliance was explicitly introduced in the Third Five Year Plan (1961-66). Self- reliance has in practice been interpreted to mean a strong import substitution orientation in the development strategy. In an extreme form self-reliance was equated with self-sufficiency which led to a position of favouring any displacement of imports by domestic production anywhere in the economy at whatever cost. The critical link between the objective of self-reliance and the import substitution orientation in the Indian strategy for industrialisation is the assumption of export pessimism.

Our vision of a self-reliant economy should be of an economy which can meet all its import requirements through exports, without undue dependence on artificial external props such as foreign aid; this is precisely the vision of self-reliance as bequeathed to us by Jawaharlal Nehru as elaborated in the Third Five Year Plan.

This factual recall suggests that India's self-reliance and import substitution were not founded on 'export pessimism' if the planners had been inclined towards outward orientation. They ought to have taken note of the only serious detailed and disaggregated empiricial analysis of Indian exports by Manmohan Singh (1964) available at the time of formulating the basic strategy for Indian industrialisation which had comprehensively established that Indian exports had been constrained by supply bottlenecks and not by demand. The strategy which formed the basis for the planning for industrialisation in India was formulated in the Second Plan (1956-61). Thus, the industrialisation strategy was settled well before 1964.

The operational issue here is the scope for the future growth of exports of labour-intensive manufactures from developing to developed countries. Given favourable demand conditions, supply bottlenecks can be overcome over a period of time. The real issue then boils down to the following: Will markets be still available if all those countries which have in the past pursued inward-looking development strategies switch over to export-oriented strategies based on labour-intensive manufactures? This is an empirical question and a reliable answer to it can have a material influence on future development strategies. At the practical level, the priority that developing countries interests are accorded in the Uruguay Round of Trade negotiations, will provide an important indication about the future of export-oriented industrialisation.

Certainly, Indian planners were not striving for an export-led development strategy, but to heap 'export pessimism' on their heads wholesale would appear to be a case of overkill. Undoubtedly, in its pursuit of import substitution, India has made quite a few errors. India has followed "a position of any displacement of imports by domestic production anywhere in the economy at whatever cost". Such a sweeping generalisation or caricaturing converts an argument into abuse for which there should be little place in a study based on highly intensive data.

Since 1950, India's industrial production has increased at an average annual rate of about 6 per cent. The country's industrial base has been greatly diversified and there has also been a considerable accumulation of scientific, technical and managerial skills. We are now self-sufficient in meeting our requirements of industrial consumer goods. We have a large diversified capital goods industry and the country has now the capacity to plan, design, set up and commission new plants for a wide range of industries such as sugar, textiles, cement, paper, steel, heavy electricals, drugs and machine tools. The reduced dependence on imported capital goods has greatly enhanced our ability to pursue an autonomous path of development, suited to the needs of our people.

The pattern of industrial growth also needs to be corrected. As stated earlier, a significant part of growth has been in consumer durables which cater to a fairly limited segment of the population. The demand for such durables and high value non-durables in absolute terms is very substantial and has come from the rapid growth in organised sector incomes. The direct and indirect foreign exchange content of meeting these demands is very high and has contributed in no small measure to the current balance of payments problems. A diversified pattern of agricultural growth and more rapid employment generation in rural areas will generate a different type of demand for manufactured goods which can be met at lower cost in terms of capital and foreign exchange. In this sense, the restructuring of industrial growth will be a consequence of the reorientation of agricultural growth referred to earlier.

The reorientation of development strategy that is being suggested will shift the focus of growth to the production of essential wage goods in preference to consumer durables. Such a shift will help in generating employment. In fact, it is a necessary requirement for an employment-oriented strategy since more rapid employment generation will tend to increase the demand for wage goods. Such a strategy will also contribute towards the generation of non-agricultural work opportunities in rural areas which will reduce urban drift and the pressure on agricultural land.

In a country like India, both, poverty and economic growth pose serious environmental challenges. Nothing can possibly be worse for environment than, say, hunger, destitution and famine. In their desperate attempt to survive today, people are forced to forsake their tomorrow and overuse their environment. A classic example of the phenomenon can be found in impoverished tribal areas where millions of households are forced to cut forests everyday and sell wood to get, at best, half-a-meal a day. And all this does not come cheaply in terms of personal costs, as foresters often tend to argue. Tribal women wake up before dawn, walk miles to the ever dwindling forests to cut and bundle wood, and then carry their heavy head load tens of kilometres to a nearby town. And after all that what they get is a pittance. At the same time uncontrolled economic growth, not just poisons and destroys cities, but also erodes the rural resource base, setting in motion a vicious cycle. Rural ecosystems, unable to support their growing populations, push more and more people into the cities.

There is, therefore, a golden mean, a balance, as in all things ecological, between poverty and wealth, between need and greed. This is an area for values, education, culture, social aspirations, human satisfaction—especially amongst those who have them in sufficient measure—in things other than what economists call goods.

The new economic policies of the government built around certain concepts of economic liberalisation and structural adjustment, have raised numerous questions in the minds of the environmentally-concerned. One set of critics believes that these policies will enhance impoverishment. Apart from being bad in itself, the policies will have a negative environmental impact. There is another set which believes that these policies will enhance entrepreneurship and processes of wealth generation, and, thus, reduce poverty. But this set too does not know how these processes will be controlled to ensure a good and clean environment. If the government could not give the country good economic governance and hence its role must now be curtailed, then, what is the guarantee that the same corrupt, inefficient, partisan and soft government, will give us good environmental governance, where the trade-offs, especially in a poor country like India, are even more difficult to assess and understand? There is, of course, another set of concerns which is as follows: even if the new policies generate wealth, will this wealth not be built on borrowed consumption patterns from industrialised countries? Will these consumption patterns not devastate our culture and environment, that is whatever that remains of them?

The rapid changes in Indian economic policies, at least partly due to the World Bank-motivated structural adjustments, have social, economic and environmental implications. Though significant amount of attention has been paid to the first two by the press and various intellectuals, the environmental implications remain, as always, neglected. Here is an attempt to rectify this neglect.

The current economic policies will have direct and indirect adverse impacts on the environment. At least some of them are not new. But perhaps the most interesting of these features can be categorised as encouraging consumerism, deregulating industry and promoting agricultural exports. Many economic policies seem directly aimed at stimulating demand and consequently, the production of consumer goods. Unfortunately, much of the attention has been focused on what are generally known as luxury items—cars, air-conditioners, refrigerators, television sets, video cassette recorders and other such items. Generally, enhanced consumerism involving production and consumption of increasing quantities of goods, and the related increase in power, water and other natural resource needs is the essence of environmentally unsustainable lifestyles. This is being acknowledged the world over and though little concrete action has emerged, there appears to be serious thinking about alternative models of development.

Despite this, in India where we can still choose, we are enthusiastically embracing the lifestyles and development models that most of the world is looking for ways to jettison. A good example is the recent reduction in the duty on cars. The explicit objective is to encourage people to buy (and use) more cars. Apart from the fact that this means import of more petroleum, it also enhances our already over-the-limit air pollution. The argument that new economic policies result in the latest, efficient, technology cannot be an adequate excuse, For, even if the new cars that come on the road are less polluting, their sheer number is enough to make the air unfit for breathing. Besides, the current economic policies do not encourage environment-friendly cars. If they were, tax relief would have been given to only those cars which met stringent fuel efficiency and pollution control standards. Nevertheless, even with the 'greenest' of cars, air pollution will continue to increase as the number of cars grow, unless of course, structural adjustment can make a car, that instead of polluting, actually cleans up the atmosphere as it cruises around! So what is needed is greater public sector investment in public transport. City and town planning has to be made conducive to lowering air pollution and encouraging more people to use the steadily improving public transport system. Instead, we are moving in the opposite direction.

Similarly, air-conditioners are made cheaper to stimulate the market. But we have little electricity and a depleting ozone layer. And much of the electricity produced is at great social and environmental costs. To feed the air-conditioners in Delhi, power is drawn from the northern grid, leaving little for the satellite towns. We already have the Rajghat and Badarpur power stations spewing tonnes of fly ash into the atmosphere. Now, a new power station is being planned at Bawana, which is upwind of Delhi and will contribute an additional three tonnes of nitrogen oxide every hour to Delhi's already polluted air.

The situation is no better in the other parts of the country. In Bombay, the Tatas are setting up a new thermal plant in the heart of the city, despite the already high air pollution levels. Another power station is coming up in Dahanu, threatening the local ecology, Madras intends to build the second phase of the North Madras power station, despite the environmental problems. Kerala hopes to feed its hungry air-conditioners by building a thermal power station in Kayamkulam and thereby ruin a valuable breeding ground for fish and prawns. The coal for this power station will come from Talcher, nearly 2,000 kms away.

Almost all the consumer items that are being promoted have significant environmental impacts. In totality, the encouragement of consumerism, as it is being done in India, is antithetical to the concept of sustainable development. With our huge and growing population and rapidly depleting natural resources, we should pioneer innovative, environmentally sustainable models of development. Instead, we are following a path that will be even more disastrous for us, than it was for its original proponents.

The survival and well-being of a nation depend on sustainable development. It is a process of social and economic betterment that satisfies the needs and values of all interest groups without foreclosing future options. To this end, we must ensure that the demand on the environment from which we derive our sustenance, does not exceed its carrying capacity for the present as well as future generations. In the past, we had a great tradition of environmental conservation which taught us to respect nature and to take cognisance of the fact that all forms of life—human, animal and plant—are closely interlinked and that disturbance in one give rise to an imbalance in other's. Even in modern times, as is evident in our constitutional provisions and environmental legislation and planning objectives, conscious efforts have been made for maintaining environmental security along with developmental advances. The Indian Constitution has laid a new important trail in the section on Directive Principles of State Policy by assigning the duties for the State and all citizens through articles 48A and 51A(g) which state that the "State shall endeavour to protect and improve the environment and to safeguard the forests and wild life, and to have compassion for the living creatures."

Nevertheless, over the years, there has been progressive pressure on the environment and the natural resources, the alarming consequences of which are becoming evident in increasing proportions. These consequences detract from the gains of development and worsen the standard of living of the poor who are directly dependent on natural resources. It is in this context that we need to give a new thrust towards conservation and sustainable development.

The National Conservation Strategy and the Policy Statement on Environment and Development are in response to the need for laying down the guidelines that will help to weave environmental considerations into the fabric of our national life and of our development process. It is an expression of our commitment for reorienting policies and action in unison with the environmental perspective.

A Bill is proposed to provide for strict liability for damages arising out of any accident occurring while handling any hazardous substance and for the establishment of a National Environment Tribunal for effective and expeditious disposal of cases arising from such accident, with a view to giving relief and compensation for damages to persons, property and the environment and for matters connected therewith or incidental thereto. Decisions were taken at the United Nations Conference on Environment and Development held at Rio de Janeiro in June, 1992, in which India participated, calling upon the States to develop national laws regarding liability and compensation for the victims of pollution and other environmental damages; and it is considered expedient to implement the decisions of the aforesaid Conference so far as they relate to the protection of environment and payment of compensation for damage to persons, property and the environment while handling hazardous substances.

Ecology is the branch of science that is concerned with the relationships of life forms with each other and with their surroundings. The basic unit in ecology is the ecosystem: a fairly self-contained system of plants and animals living in a particular kind of environment. A forest is an ecosystem; so is a lake. Every ecosystem has four elements: (*i*) the non-living environment, (*ii*) producers, (*iii*) consumers, and (*iv*) decomposers.

Pollution is generally defined as an undersirable and excessive addition of substance to water, air and land which adversely alters the natural quality of the environment. The term environment includes the land, air and water. No pollution is inevitable and measures to prevent pollution or reduce its effects have grown rapidly in recent times. Action against pollution takes a variety of forms. Most countries including India have anti-pollution legislation. Recycling of materials may be done; for example, glass bottles, newspaper, metals from old cars can all be recycled. There can be research into the use of cleaner, renewable sources of energy, for example, solar, wind and tidal energy. Modification of industrial processes to make use of waste materials, or to render them harmless before discharge, is another anti-pollution measure.

Finally, environmental considerations should be integrated while encouraging industrial growth. The action points in this regard should include a mix of promotional and regulatory steps which may be listed as follows:

(*i*) Incentives for environmentally clean technologies, recycling and reuse of wastes and conservation of natural resources;

(*ii*) Operationalisation of "polluter pays principle" by introducing effluent tax, resources for industry and implementation of standards based on resource consumption and production capacity;

(*iii*) Fiscal incentives to small-scale industries for pollution control and for reduction of wastes;

(*iv*) While deciding upon site, priority to compatible industries so that, to the extent possible, wastes from one could be used as raw material for the other and thus the net pollution load is minimised;

(*v*) Location of industries as per environmental guidelines for siting of industry;

(*vi*) Enforcement of pollution control norms in various types of industrial units depending on their production processes/ technologies and pollution potential; particular attention to be paid to highly polluting industries;

(*vii*) Encouragement for use of environmentally benign automobiles/ motor vechicles and reduction of auto-emissions;

(*viii*) Collective efforts for installation and operation of common effluent treatment facilities in industrial estates and in areas with a cluster of industries;

(*ix*) Introduction of "Environmental Audit" and reports thereof to focus on environment related policies, operations and activities in industrial concern with specific reference to pollution control and waste management;

(*x*) Dissemination of information for public awareness on environmental safety aspects and stringent measures to ensure safety of workers and general population against hazardous substances and processes;

(*xi*) Preparation of on-site emergency plans for hazardous industries and off-site emergency plans for districts in which hazardous units are located;

(*xii*) Public liability insurance against loss or injury to life or property;

(*xiii*) Setting up of environment cells in industries for implementing environmental management plans and for compliance of the requisites of environmental laws;

(*xiv*) Internalising the environmental safeguards as integral component of the total project cost;

(*xv*) Environmental impact assessment from the planning stage and selection of site for location of industries; and

(xvi) Clearance by Ministry of Environment and Forests of all projects above a certain size and in certain fragile areas.

10

India's Dwindling Forests: A Threat to Environment and Eco-System

K.P. Nath

Forests in India are fast disappearing seriously degrading her environment and disturbing her eco-system. With tremendous growth of population and large scale industrialisation during the recent years, there has been indiscriminate felling of trees for timber, fuel and fodder. To feed factories with bamboos and trees for paper, plywood and packing boxes, many forests have virtually vanished. Advancing villages are encroaching upon lands that were once under forest cover. Forests are being cleared for reclamation as agricultural lands. Villages are being established on lands close to forests and forest lands are being used as grazing grounds for domestic cattle.

It has been estimated that for maintaining proper ecological balance in nature at least 33 per cent of total land area should be under forest cover. In India forest land which was previously calculated to be 22.8 per cent of the total land area is now confirmed to be as low as 18 per cent through satellite survey as against 29 per cent in the world. This is also not safe from illegal intrusion. Thinning of forests continues unabated with indiscriminate felling of trees. The tropical rain forests of the Western Ghats have already disappeared. The foot-hills of the Satpura and the Aravalli ranges have yielded to the axemen. Bare mounds stand in their place. Once a natural forest is denuded through excessive exploitation, growing of new plants there becomes difficult, because losing the natural humidity as provided by surrounding trees, the earth becomes dry and parched. The long east-west stretch of forests in the foot-hills of the Himalayas now faces the same plight.

In the north-eastern region of India, the home-land of a myriad variety of hill-tribes, jhumming of land for agriculture (a slash and burn method of cultivation) is practised. With population rapidly growing there, faster at any rate than in the plains, more hill slopes are being brought under jhumming every year. This is how forest land in the north-eastern region of India is also shrinking very fast. As hills become bare from protective forest cover, erosion of land during the rainy season becomes rampant in this region. The soil carried by streams and rivulets get deposited in the river-beds of the plains causing frequent flood during rainy season.

In western India, losing all their vegetation, the Aravalli ranges have further intensified the desert condition that already prevails there. The Thar desert is advancing at a rapid pace and is about to engulf the whole of Rajasthan. The Satpura ranges with their bare hills have intensified drought conditions in Maharashtra and Madhya Pradesh. People there suffer from acute hardship due to drought in dry summer season. Miles after miles the land gets parched. Rainy season there has become shorter and rainfall irregular and sparse.

By losing their natural habitats in forests, a myriad varieties of India's flora and fauna are disappearing very fast. The loss is irreparable. There are also illegal poachers who wantonly kill rare species of wild animals and birds and thus threaten their very existence on earth.

To prevent our environment from deteriorating further we have to preserve whatever forests we still have from further destruction. A vigorous attempt of afforestation has to be made. For maintaining ecological balance in nature, we must without further delay develop and follow a firm national policy towards preservation of forests. For every one hectare of forest land made bare, ten hectares should be brought under forest cover. This is necessary for our very survival on earth.

Introduction

Forests in India are fast shrinking. Many forests have virtually vanished due to overexploitation by people for food, fodder, fuel and timber. Villages are being established, road built and paddy field extended by clearing forests. Increasing population demands more land for agriculture which can only be obtained by clearing forests. Along with growing human population in rural India, cattle population is also increasing. To meet the ever increasing demand for food every piece of available land is being brought under cultivation leaving less and less grazing ground for cattle every year. To solve the problem of grazing, cattle are driven inside forests for pasture. As advancing villages are now well nigh the fringe of forests, cowherds with their cattle have easy access to them. The young seedlings and saplings that naturally grow inside forests are either devoured or trampled down by the cattle while foraging thereby strongly checking the regeneration potential of forests. Further, the grazing cattle loosen the top soil inside forests with their hooves. Thus the precious top soil of forests which required thousands of years to form gets washed away during rains within a few years. Grazing, particularly uncontrolled over-grazing of cattle is, therefore, one of the prominent reasons for forest degradation. Over and above these, leaves are plucked and branches cut to provide to cattle as fodder at a rate far more than forests can actually recuperate.

The rural poor are more dependent on forests than the urban rich for their daily needs. All house building materials of the rural poor—the pole, the cane and the bamboos are collected from nearby forests.

Tender plants, before they could grow into big trees, are cut to use as poles and beams in house building. Big trees which have already become scarce in forests of the plain regions of India are felled and sawn into timber for doors, windows, ceilings and furniture. The rural poor are also dependent on firewood from forests for their daily cooking. Gas, electricity, coke coal, kerosene, etc., for cooking have not found way into rural households mainly because of the unaffordable cost involved in their use. Forests have been foraged for fire-wood so much so that these have lost capacity to regenerate. As villages advance, forests in their vicinity recede resulting in the scarcity of for fire-wood even in rural areas. As an alternative to fire-wood, cow-dung, which could otherwise be used as manure to fertilise the field, is now being dried and increasingly used in oven for cooking. As a result fertility of the field is falling and rural farmers are becoming increasingly dependent on artificial fertilisers and insecticides to keep up crop yield. Artificial fertilisers and insecticides may be good to boost up crop production, but these have harmful effects on fish, birds and man himself. Fish either die or get diseased by taking these fertilisers and insecticides washed into rivers and ponds. These insecticides ultimately find way into the stomach of birds and man through fish.

In rural areas along with fire-wood, cow-dung has also become a scarce commodity. After a day's forage deep into forests women will return home with a fagot of wood on their head in the evening walking a few kilometres when cow-dung will not be available for cooking as there is always keen competition in collecting it from the cattle's grazing ground. This has caused wanton destruction of forests.

Fields and forests everywhere are overgrazed with the result that these lose capacity to recuperate. With the cover of grass and shrubs gone, topsoil becomes bare and gets washed away with rainwater. The earth thereby becomes barren. Overexploitation of forests have left them largely diminished in size. At places forests have virtually vanished.

Besides firewood and timber, rapid industrialisation has created demands for bamboo, tree-logs and other forest products for manufacturing paper, plywood and planks for packing boxes. Lush green tropical rain forests of India have already yielded to the axe, saw and bulldozer of greedy man ever seeking commercial gains through exploitation of the natural vegetation of the earth. The result is unprecedented change of weather and drought condition which cause untold hardship to people every year. Industrialisation has led us to such a pass that it has become difficult for us to choose between economic development and environment protection.

It has been estimated that for maintaining proper ecological balance in nature at least 33 per cent of the total land area should be under forest cover. Today, approximately 29 per cent of the total land area of the world has remained under forest. In India forest land was previously calculated to be 22.8 per cent of the total land area. Now an aerial survey with the help of the satellite confirms the figure to be as low as 19.47 per cent.[1] This is also not safe from illegal intrusion. Thinning of forests continues unabated with indiscriminate felling of trees. The tropical rain forests of the Western Ghats have already disappeared. The foot-hills of the Satpura and the Aravalli ranges have yielded to the axemen. Bare mounds stand in their place. Once a natural forest is denuded through excessive exploitation, growing of new plants there becomes difficult, because losing the natural humidity as provided by surrounding trees, the earth becomes dry and parched. The long east-west stretch of forests in the foot-hills of the Himalayas now faces the same plight. Denuded of forests the hills have become bare and consequently erosion-prone. Soil washed away by rainwater gets deposited in the river bed of the Ganga and its tributaries causing them to swell up thereby reducing their capacity to hold river water during the rains. The result is frequent flood in Uttar Pradesh and Bihar hiring the rainy seasons.

The north-eastern region of India is the abode of diverse hill tribes. All of them practise jhumming, a method of cultivation in which the forests are cleared by slashing plants and shrubs. These are then left to dry for about a month. Before the onset of rains the dry leaves, twigs and branches are set ablaze. When rain water washes away the ashes leaving the earth soft and bare, people grow there maize, vegetables and paddy. As the population in the hills is rapidly growing, faster at any rate than in the plains, more and more hill slopes are being brought under jhumming every year. Also to enable to recuperate the fertility of land, the place of cultivation is shifted every three or four years. As a result, no tree can grow over a large tract of hilly land. This is how the forest land in the north-eastern region of India is also shrinking very fast. As the hills become bare from the protective cover of forests, erosion of land during the rainy season becomes rampant in this region. The soil carried by streams and rivulets gets deposited in the river-beds in the plains of Assam causing frequent flood during rainy season there.

In western India, losing all their vegetations, the Aravalli ranges have further intensified the desert condition that already prevails there. The Thar desert is advancing at a rapid pace and is about to engulf the whole of Rajasthan. Similarly, the Satpura range with their bare hills have intensified drought condition in Maharashtra and Madhya Pradesh. People there suffer from acute hardship due to drought in dry summer season. Miles after miles the land gets parched. Rainy season there has become shorter and rainfall irregular and sparse.

By losing their natural habitats in forests a myriad variety of India's flora and fauna are disappearing very fast. The loss is irreparable. There are also illegal hunters and poachers who wantonly kill rare species of wild animals and birds and thus threaten their very existence on earth. We are as if precariously placed on the branch of a tree the root of which we are cutting for our downfall on earth along with the branch.

To prevent our environment from deteriorating further we have to preserve whatever forests we still have from further destruction. A vigorous attempt of afforestation in wastelands, bare hilly lands, on both sides of highways and railways, on the boundaries of city parks and other public places, in school, hospital and office compounds has to be made. Every householder whether in villages, towns or cities should be encouraged to plant trees on their lands. For maintaining ecological balance in nature, we must without further delay firmly follow the national policy towards preservation of forests. For every one hectare of forest land made bare, ten hectares should be brought under forest cover. This is necessary for our very survival on earth.

Some Grim Facts

With less than 2 per cent of the total forest area of the world, our country supports 15 per cent of the world's population. Our population increased from 361 million in 1951 to nearly 844 million in 1991, while the per capita forest area decreased from 0.20 hectare to 0.10 hectare during that very period.[2]

India has less than 0.50 per cent of the pastures of the world, but its livestock population constitutes more than 13 per cent of the world's estimated 3 billion heads of domesticated animals. As of now, over 90 million animals graze in our forests which cannot support even half that number.[3]

Even though 47 per cent of the total land area of our country is under agriculture (very high as compared to many other countries), land hunger is far from satisfied. 4.35 million hectares of forest land is subject to shifting cultivation and 0.7 million hectares (as per record) of forest land has been encroached upon for permanent cultivation.[4] Although forest land is being reclaimed and brought under agriculture, per capita cultivable land is declining. It has declined from 0.48 hectare in 1951 to

0.26 hectare in 1981. It is apprehended that by the year 2000 A.D., it will go further down to around 0.11 hectare per capita.[5]

Rapid loss of forests was evidenced during the two decades from 1960 to 1980 in most developing countries. India lost 4.8 million hectares of her tropical rain forests as against 1.15 million hectares in Myanmar (Burma) and 5.26 million hectares in Indonesia.[6] India is currently losing her forests at the rate of 1.5 million hectares a year.[7] Projections by some observers suggest that if this deforestation trend continues, much of the remaining tropical forests would be cleared by the end of the present century. India like her neighbours, Sri Lanka and Bangladesh, has already lost nearly all her primary forests.[8] The total recorded forest area of the country which had been 78.396 million hectares in 1959-60 has come down to 74.960 million hectares by 1975.[9] Around this time the National Commission on Agriculture (NCA) coined the term 'social forestry' for forestry development activities on non-forest public as well as individually owned lands.

Over the past decade many State Forest Departments in India have come to realise that survival of protected areas of forests depends ultimately on the support of the local people rather than fences, fines and even armed forces. A number of promising projects have been initiated by government and non-government organisations to reduce pressure on forests by alleviating poerty in communities living in or near forest areas. In Andhra Pradesh, for example, solar cookers were distributed to tribals living in forests to minimise their dependence on fuelwood. But these tribals instead of using them sold them away for luxury goods. Unless people are made to realise the utility of solar cooker through frequent demonstration, it is difficult to wean them of their traditional mode of cooking with fuelwood.[10]

In India, apart from the use of fuelwood for cooking, among the rural poor, lack of adequate grazing ground has also led to the loss of forests. The nation's 12 million hectares of permanent pasture are vastly inadequate to the needs of its 196 million heads of cattle. Grazing ground, crucial to the animals of the poor, has shrunk by about one-fourth over the past forty years. Forests, roadsides and fallow lands make up the fodder deficit. But most cows still go hungry and the pressure on the forest grows.[11]

Several nations like Bhutan, Botswana, Czechoslovakia (former), Panama, Venezuela and Chile have over 15 per cent of their lands designated as parks.[12] In comparison to these countries, India provides for 4.18 per cent of her total land area as parks and sanctuaries, lower than the world average of 4.9 per cent, with all her 74 national parks and 411 widlife sanctuaries.[13]

Depletion of forests has caused heavy accumulation of carbon-dioxide in air. Carbon-dioxide content in air was fairly stable till the end of the nineteenth century. It started rising thereafter. Increased burning of fossil fuels like coal in factories, furnaces and locomotives and petrol and diesel in aircrafts and automobiles have polluted air particularly in industrial towns and cities almost to the point of suffocation causing chronic ailments of eye, throat, heart and lung. Delhi is one of the highly polluted cities of the world. Trees and plants absorb carbon-dioxide from the air through their green leaves and release oxygen into air by means of 'photo-synthesis' and thus act as a great sink for atmospheric carbon-dioxide. Environmentalists have estimated that almost one-third of the carbon-dioxide content present in air today is because of the wanton depletion of forests.[14] Now carbon-dioxide is one of the greenhouse gases responsible for the warming of the earth. It has been estimated that due to steady build up of carbon-dioxide and methane (another greenhouse gas) in air the temperature of the earth is slowly rising. It is likely that within the next fortyfive years, that is during the life time of today's young adults, the earth's average temperature will go up by as much as 3 degrees Celsius.[15] This will bring in its trail many disastrous consequences. Rise in the earth's mean temperature will cause ice in the Arctic and the Antarctic regions to melt. Sea level will thereby rise inundating many low lying coastal areas reducing further the per capita available land for agriculture which is already steadily declining due to uncontrolled population growth. Per capita production of foodgrain will consequently be less perpetuating hunger, malnutrition and disease. To avert this and other ecological disasters that will befall on us in the foreseeable future, it is high time that we act in right earnest to increase our forest land.

While the national forest policy stipulates that the land under forests should have a coverage of one-third of the geographical area, the national average of forest coverage is estimated to be around 22 per cent. The crucial issue before us is, therefore, how to increase forest land so as to reach the level of 33 per cent of the total geographical area of the country.

Measures to be Adopted

Population in India is increasing at a galloping speed. Deforestation and its concomitant ills like air pollution and ecological imbalance in nature are the direct consequence of population explosion. As a first measure for the solution of the problem of deforestation, population growth in India must be drastically checked. The rate of growth of population must be brought down to the level that exists at present in most European countries. When the present rate of growth of population is 2.34 per cent per year in India, over a dozen countries in Europe have long achieved a zero or near zero growth rate. Some European countries like Germany, Hungary and Denmark have even achieved a negative growth rate. To be at par with these countries, India must adopt a stricter population control policy than it is now. All government employees at first instance must adopt a one-child family norm if they are to enjoy facilities like leave travel concessions, medical reimbursement and house building advances. Maternity leave in case of married female employees must be stopped after the birth of one child. No citizen should be allowed to contest election and hold office if he or she has more than two children which should be later brought down to one. Persons seeking job under the government must give an undertaking that they will adopt one-child family norm and stand the risk of losing job for violation of this norm at any time. Delayed marriage and celebacy should be encouraged with incentives. Various birth control devices should be made available and popularised. Compulsory sterilisation of either couple having more than two children should be enforced. Population growth in India and consequent dwindling of forests can be checked by adopting such measures.

Vigorous attempts should be made by mobilising both individuals and non-governmental agencies for growing trees on fallow lands and waste lands under the scheme of social forestry started by various State Governments. Individual farmers should be encouraged to adopt agro-forestry on their farm land so as to be doubly benefitted, periodically with foodgrains and crops and perennially with fruits, fuel, fodder and timber from the same agricultural field. If both the social forestry and agro-forestry schemes can be widely implemented, pressure on forests can be substantially reduced.

Cattle population in villages should be kept under control. Farmers should be encouraged to rear a few healthy, productive breeds of cattle rather than many sickly and unproductive ones. Co-operative dairy farming should be encouraged so that improved varieties of cows are reared at one place in a scientific manner for maximising the production of milk.

Better and durable substitutes of timber should be found out through extensive research and their use popularised in house building and furniture making.

Paper manufacturers should be given to cultivate bamboo in wide stretches of lands to feed their mills with. Waste papers should be recycled to minimise the use of bamboo. At least one third of the paper produced should be from the recycled waste papers.

Tree plantation in a massive manner should be started on government lands, in all government run organisations, hospitals, primary health centres, maternity homes, schools and office premises.

The eco-system in nature is not vastly resilient. Unless the rate at which forests are being destroyed is reversed with massive afforestation, it is apprehended that nature's system of maintaining ecological equilibrium will be permanently damaged. Mother earth's ability to sustain life on her lap will then be adversely affected. If we do not come forward adopting corrective measures right now, what is today's threat will be tomorrow's catastrophe.

REFERENCES

1. Forest Survey of India (1989): *The Stale of Forestry Report*, 25, Subhash Road, Dehradun, p. 20.
2. Khullar, Pankaj (1992): Forestry Programmes: Need for Change in Approach. *The Indian Forester*, Vol. 118, No. 10, October, p. 737.
3. *Ibid.*
4. *Ibid.*
5. Jha, L.K. & Nath K.P., Population, Resource Availability, Environment and Agroforestry, Jha, L.K. (ed.). *Agroforestry*, Ashis Publishing House, New Delhi, p. 17
6. Barraclough, S. & Ghimire, K. (1990): *The Social Dynamics of Deforestation in Developing Countries*, United Nations Research Institute for Social Development (UNRISD), Discussion Paper 16, November, p. 8.
7. Postel, Sandra & Ryan, John C. (1991): Reforming Forestry, *State of the World*, Worldwatch Institute, New Delhi, p. 77.
8. Barraclough, S., & Ghimire, K., *op. cit.*, p. 9.
9. Sammugasundaram, S. (1992): Forestry: Issues and State of Art, *The Indian Forester*, Vol. 118, No. 10, October, p. 718.
10. Khullar, Pankaj, *op. cit.*, p. 742.
11. Durning, Alan Thein & Brough, Holly B. (1992): Reforming the Livestock Economy, *The State of the World*, Worldwatch Institute, New Delhi, p. 73.

12. Ryan, John C. (1992): Conserving Biological Diversity, *State of the World*, Worldwatch Institute, New Delhi, p. 15.
13. Singh, R.L. (1991): Wildlife Conservation and Economic Development Programme—A Case Study, *The Indian Forester*, Vol. 117, No. 10, October, p. 804.
14. Shrinking Woods, *India Today*, June 15, 1992, p. 82.
15. Brown, Lester R. (1985): A False Sense of Security, *The State of the World*, Worldwatch Institute Report, Prentice Hall of India (P) Ltd., New Delhi, p. 16.

11

Property Rights, the Hills and the Tragedy of the Commons in Manipur

Amar. S. Yumnam

Manipur is a land of interesting contrasts for a student of development economics. Here the hills occupy nine-tenths of the total land area and the remaining constitutes the plain valley areas. Whereas most of the population settle in the valley which is where most of the economic activities take place, in the hills shifting cultivation is still practised. Besides, the land laws establishing private property rights in land are operational in the valley area, while the traditional more or less communal ownership system is still prevalent in these areas. Efforts to extend the individual property rights in the hills are encountered with stiff opposition from the hill people. These contrasts have thrown up many important development issues relating to land, group interests, environment and location of economic activity. This paper is an attempt to highlight some of the issues involved.

Introduction

India is a vast country with its different regions having different socio-economic, political and physical characteristics and widely divergent initial conditions when planning for economic development first started in the country. Now most of the major problems facing the country have their roots in the irrational approach to planning India adopted in the beginning wherein an attempt was made to identify and solve a common national problem. India never had and will never have a common single problem; its different regions will continue to face divergent socio-economic problems. Any effort to reduce India to a single micro or macro problem will always be a disaster. The purpose of this paper is to explain the process through which the rich forest resources of Manipur were brought to their present pathetic state.

Manipur: *A Backgrounder:* Manipur, a small province in the north-east corner of India, is a veritable land of interesting contrasts for a student of development economics. Its total geographical area of 22,327 sq. kms. consists of two clear-cut topographical divisions—rows of hills around and a small valley in the middle. The hills, corresponding to five administrative districts, cover an area of 20,089 sq. kms. or 89.98 per cent of the total land area. The small valley in the middle of the province, corresponding to the remaining three districts out of eight, covers an area of 2,238 sq. kms. or 10.02 per cent of the total land area. But the population distribution pattern is just the reverse of the geographical area. As of 1991 census, 1,177,480 or 64.46 per cent of the total population of 1,825,714 persons were residents in the small valley area and the rest 649,234 or 35.54 per cent in the hills. The density of population works out, according to the same census, to 32 persons per sq. km. in the hills and 562 persons per sq. km. in the valley compared to the all-India average of 267 persons per sq. km. This density ranges from 20 to 63 persons per sq. km. in the five hill districts and 363 to 576 persons in the three valley districts. In keeping with the population distribution pattern, most of the economic activities also take place in the small valley area. The population in the hills consists mainly of the economically weaker and socially more backward tribal groups, while the composition in the valley is a mixed one.

Property Rights System: *A Primer*: Another interesting feature distinguishing the hills from the valley is the property rights system prevailing in the two. In the valley, a tradition of private property rights system has been firmly established though there still remains many intricate issues to be settled. But in the hills, it is an entirely different picture. The 29 different ethnic groups living in the hills are classified into two main tribal groups—the Nagas and the Kukis. These two communities have *prima facie* two types of property rights system in land.[1]

Naga Property Rights System: In the Naga group of tribes, the community ownership of land is stressed. The entire village land belongs either to the chief or the community as a whole. But there are certain cultivable lands where the individuals/clans enjoy inalienable rights so long as the ownership of these are not transferred to people from outside the village. If any transfer of these lands are to be affected, prior approval of the village administration is called for.

The land use pattern of the Nagas has certain clear-cut divisions. First, they have the house-site where the villagers settle and construct their houses. Secondly, surrounding this house-site, there is a protected forest area where no felling of trees, etc., are allowed. This protective area serves as a defensive wall for the village against fire and other attacks to the village. Beyond this defensive area, they have their cultivable areas where individuals/clans are given ownership. The plotless farmers can hire these plots for cultivation on payment of rent per cultivating year.

Kuki Property Rights System: Unlike among the Nagas, the prerogative of the chief is accepted to a great extent among the Kukis.[2] The chief has overriding power over the use of the village land. In fact, he is the owner of the village land. Nevertheless, every villager is assured a cultivable plot of land. This applies even in the case of the immigrant who has been accepted by the village chief as a co-villager.

All the villagers will have to pay tributes in paddy to the chief out of the total annual harvests and in accordance with the terms and conditions of the oral lease between the chief and the villager entered into in the beginning of the season. But all these do not constitute a transfer of property rights to the villager from the chief. Once the jhum cycle is over, the ownership and possession of the land necessarily reverts back to the chief. The same process is replicated even in cases where the chief acquires new land, establishes a village there and invites his near and dear ones to settle therein. To put in short, communal land ownership system prevails among the Kukis but with the chief serving as the guardian and benefactor of the village and as the person responsible for the maintenance of the customs, laws and traditions of the community.

Common Features: From the above brief picture, we can discern certain common features of land ownership systems in both the communities. There are: (a) Among the Nagas, the community exercises overall control over the village land but the individuals are given certain inalienable rights in so far as the ownership of the cultivable areas is concerned; and (b) Among the Kukis, the chief has inalienable rights of ownership over the land and exercises control over it, but he at the same time sees to it that the villagers get proper plots of land for cultivation and are assured their livelihood. So in both the communities the property rights system is governed by traditional unwritten laws and conventions. In both, the system boils down to more or less a community ownership system where the individuals enjoy higher rights among the Nagas while the chief exercises greater power among the Kukis. Both these are quite contrary to the fairly well established private land ownership system prevailing in the valley where the Manipur Land Revenue and Land Reforms Act, 1960 is fully operational. What should be of grave concern to all is the recent phenomenon of emergence of landless individuals and families in both the communities despite the prevalence of more or less communal land ownership system. This implies the collapse of the traditional system without a commensurate emergence of an alternative one. This is particularly pathetic and unfortunate for the poor and the forests.

Farming System in the Hills: Irrespective of the community, jhuming or shifting cultivation is the most widely prevalent form of farming; terrace cultivation is not yet widely established for reasons of economy or otherwise. The political economy aspect of this is the least researched area. As yet no accurate or systematic data are available on this practice, perhaps to the great advantage of the people earning profits from the forests. It is, however, estimated that 1,00,000 hectares of land are subject to this cultivation; out of this 60,000 hectares are shown at any point of time in the jhum cycle. It is reported that about 40-50 years back, the jhum cycle extended beyond ten years, but now this is less than five years. It would be in place to bring in here the picture of forests, the tribals and the hills from the interconnectedness angle. A land area of 15,021 sq. kms. or 67.27 per cent of the total land area of the province is classified as forest area. Almost all of this is in the hills. What is most alarming is that 14,301 sq. kms. or 95.21 per cent of this forest area were found to be degraded forests or scrub land by a survey in 1990.[3]

Tragedy of the Commons: *First Reasons:* This vast as well as fast depletion of forest resources is having economy-wide serious environmental and social consequences. One of the serious debates going on in the province is the survival of the biggest fresh water lake in Eastern India and situated in the valley, the Loktak, which is now threatened by siltation consequent upon the depletion of the forests in the hills. Now what is of utmost interest to a researcher is the political economy behind the blaming of shifting cultivation as the only reason responsible for forest denudation.[4] But it is highly doubtful if this official reason is a major, leave aside the sole, factor responsible for forest degradation. But before we take issue with this reasoning, it would be in place to accept the property rights system in the hills as first explanations of forest degradations in Manipur.

The land property rights system in both the communities has a tragedy of the commons aspect inherent in them. Among the Nagas, the individuals do not have the incentive to invest in land for the land ultimately belongs to the community. Among the Kukis too, the land suffers from the same fate for the land ultimately belongs to the chief. This unfortunate feature is accentuated by the fact that the elites among the tribals do not feel the necessity nor do have the willingness to invest in the hills for two reasons. First, the prevailing system provides them unlimited access to the resources in the hills. Secondly, it serves their interests better if they invest their resources in the valley where a strong foundation for private property rights system has been established, evident from the recent increase in the number of settlement colonies of both the communities in the valley. In other words, the better off in both the communities are enjoying the best of both the worlds. Further, the prevailing system serves the purpose of the forest contractors and the government forest officials in enriching themselves though at heavy social costs in that they can easily exploit the invaluable forest resources by just satisfying the chief.

We should, however, hasten to add that the shifting cultivation cannot be a major cause of environmental or forest degradation in the hills. To begin with, the density of population in the hills is quite low. Secondly, the areas estimated to the under shifting cultivation is only about 5 per cent of the total land area of the hills. Thirdly, not all the forest area in the hills is suitable for shifting cultivation. Fourthly, forest degradation is occurring even in areas where felling of trees is legally prohibited. Lastly, the jhum cultivation area per cultivating household works out to less than one hectare, which is too low to cause a major environmental disaster.

Tragedy of the Commons: *Ultimate Causes:* In the circumstances prevailing in the province, it would be naive to try to explain the environmental degradation by a single reason. It is a concatenation of various factors which is at work. When planning was started in the country, the region definitely had a quite different set of initial conditions as compared to the picture of the country as a whole.[5] Since the initial conditions were vastly different and also since the necessity and significance of planning were not yet fully appreciated by the masses, planning in such circumstances was a veritable challenge and should be able to break through the initial inertia. This can be done only by a big push which creates maximum of externalities and thereby fosters a new momentum of development rather than the old low level trap.[6] But this unfortunately did not happen in the province.

Secondly, the planning efforts were based on an ideology of establishing an exchange mechanism based on commercial principles rather than one based on production. This is a fall-out of the attempt to reduce the problems of India into a common single one. The new exchange mechanism sought to be established was very alien to the traditional exchange relationships prevailing in the province, particularly in the hills, and it disturbed the traditional tranquil equilibrium without establishing a new one.

The consequence of the half-hearted and confused planning has been the emergence into pre-eminence of the rent seeking attitude in the economy and society today. In this atmosphere, the worse-off sections of the society could not enjoy any crumbs from the planning efforts of the government.[7] But they did experience the 'demonstration effect' though they did not have the resources to afford it. So, the only alternative open to them, particularly the hilly populace, was to resort to the exploitation of forest resources, much against their will, tradition and beliefs. Here again, the poor did not get the full benefits of it. The better off and the middle men took full advantage of it for the poor did not have the skill nor the access to the newly created exchange mechanism. So even for minor needs, a huge exploitation of the forest resources was to be resorted to Consequently, the forests suffered.

Market Tragedies: *On the Way:* In these circumstances, a new policy of privatisation and liberalisation is being pursued in India now. This new policy has its own exigencies and rationality. But in so far as the tribal life and the hills are concerned, it is only going to add market tragedies to the planning failures discussed earlier. The earlier planning efforts had utterly failed to provide any foundation for a long term development of the province nor could it ensure any sustainable means of livelihood to the tribal population in particular. But now the people have to fend for themselves in the market place. This is going to be, as before, a very unfair kind of relationship given the fact that the tribals do not have any resource of their own except the forests. So in order to sustain themselves, they will continue denuding the forests and thereby leading to further environmental degradation. In other words, the new policy framework will be environmentally disastrous for the province and will worsen the condition of the tribals further. Here again, the tribals are going to suffer a double squeeze. First, their only resource, forests, will get depleted further at a fast rate under the increasing pressure of the forest contractors and the tribal elites in collusion with the government forest officials. On the other hand, they will have increasingly to resort to the denudation of the forests just to maintain their present condition.

In conclusion, it must be said that the problems being faced in the province, particularly in the hills, are not simple and cannot be analysed from the perspective of mainland India. Many social, financial and technological issues are tangled up. What is required at present is to develop an efficient and equitable road transport system,[8] a strategy for ensuring food and energy availability, a clear-cut forest-*cum*-environment policy,[9] and a rational property rights legislation. But we wonder if all these can be achieved through the market forces.

---

* The paper has benefitted from the author's short stay in France in 1994 with the Masion des Sciences de l'Homme as the Host.

REFERENCES

1. What is being narrated is only a general picture, for the property rights system in land differs in details even between adjoining villages, though the residents belong to the same group.
2. Burman, B.K. Roy (1986): *Community Land and Institutional Finance (With Reference to Tribal Areas of Manipur and Tripura)*, Council for Social Development, New Delhi.
3. State Remote Sensing Centre, Department of Science, Technology and Environment and National Remote Sensing Agency, Department of Space, Government of India (1990): *Report on Land Use/Land Cover: Manipur Stale*, Imphal/Hyderabad, Table 2.
4. Government of India (1976): *Report of the National Commission on Agriculture, Part XIII, Employment and Special Area Programmes*, Ministry of Agriculture and Irrigation New Delhi, Planning Commission (1977): *Report on the Development of the North Eastern Region: Some Aspects*, New Delhi, p. 45: National Committee on the Development of Backward Areas (1981): *Report on Development of North Eastern Region*, Planning Commission, New Delhi, Chapter 5.
5. For an elaborate discussion on this, see the same author's "*Economic Development of the North-Eastern Region of India: Performance and Policy Issues*", Unpublished Ph. D. Thesis, University of Bombay, Bombay, 1985.
6. For a recent powerful exposition of the big push theory, see Murphy, Kevin, Schleifer, Andrei and Vishny, Rohert (1991): "Industrialisation and the Big Push' ', *Journal of Political Economy.*
7. On planning and rent seeking attitude in the province, see the same author's "Planning for Development in Manipur", Paper read in the State Level Seminar on Planning for Eradication of Poverty and Unemployment in Manipur, April, 1991.
8. On this, see the author's "Road Transport in Manipur: towards a framework for an efficient and equitable growth", Working Paper, Department of Economics, Manipur University, 1991, Reprinted in *Regional Integration*, Vol. XIX, 1994.
9. For a general discussion on environment and development, see Christensen, Paul P. (1989): "Historical roots for ecological economics—biophysical *versus* allocative approaches", *Ecological Economics*, Vol. 1, pp. 17-36: and Soderbaum, Peter (1992): "Neoclassical and institutional approaches to development and the environment", *Ecological Economics*, Vol. 5, pp. 127-144.

12

Sustainability of Development: Economic and Environmental Study of a Village

K. Nageswara Rao

The present study highlights the ecological and environmental impact of irrigation development, as it is practised in drought prone areas, with specific reference to Atmakur, a village in Anantapur district of Andhra Pradesh in India.

Until 1950s two percolation tanks were effective in collecting run-off water and maintaining the water table in the dug wells. Later this common property of the village became private property. For over three decades now these percolation tanks have only huge bunds which are the public property and tank beds which are 'patta' private land.

The gravity of this process of privatisation of public property was not fully realised until the late 1970s when yet another private entrepreneurial zeal set a process that now threatens the very survival of the village economy. And this is related to the ground water exploitation for irrigation.

With the given rainfall and deliberate encroachment upon the percolation tanks in favour of private gain of a few individuals, the crux of the scarcity of water in the village depends entirely on the behaviour of exploitation of ground water by wells. This resulted in drying up of dug wells and the villages witnessed serious drinking water problem by the end of 1980s. Later, the technology of in-well bores and the state policy of fixing flat rate tariff for agriculture proved disastrous. The water table is depleting so fast that a few in-well bores have dried up leading to a grave ecological and environmental threat to the very sustenance of human, animal and plant life of the village.

The entire village therefore has a single season crop area in Kharif. The cropping pattern experienced rapid changes—jowar the major crop is replaced by groundnut. The tamarind trees in the village commons have started drying up in the recent years. As a result, people started moving out of the village in search of livelihood. The vital statistics of the village revealed that between 1971 and 1981 census the rate of growth of population has been less than the national average and the slowing down of the growth of workforce indicating the possibility of migration.

Thus, Atmakur is a clear and conspicuous case of gross neglect of surface water and overexploitation of ground water, causing severe and potent irreversible environmental and ecological degradation of resources and deprivation of livelihood activities to the people. Therefore, it is a clear evidence of man-made hazard in the absence of protecting institutional system. The question therefore is how to make development sustainable in the sense of not only providing for the basic needs of the present and future generations of people in these areas but also for improvement of their quality of life?

I

Many Third World countries had set themselves on a resource-intensive path for development. This has been a path that grossly ignored the non-linearity of development and in some countries the slow-down started in the mid-sixties and "the uprooting and dispossesing effects" of this strategy started becoming visible.[1] In recent years, in some countries the situation has turned into a series of crises. To quote the World Commission on Environment and Development "over half of all developing countries actually experienced declining per capita gross domestic product in the years 1982-85 and per capita GDP has fallen for developing countries as a whole by around 10 per cent in 1980s".

As a part of the technocratic, resource-intensive strategy, irrigation programme had devastating impact in the form of degradation and destruction of resources like forests, soil, etc., and the displacement and deprivation of the dependent people with development of irrigation. Though the ecological impact of major storage dams are well documented, with a few exceptions, there are hardly any studies on the impact of irrigation policy and practice in the drought-prone areas. And this in spite of the fact that in countries like India forty per cent of the cultivated area are and one-sixth of the population live in dry and drought-prone areas. Just as these areas miss the priorities of planned investment, so they miss the researchers who are always after investment.

The present note is an attempt to highlight the ecological impact of irrigation 'development' as it is practised in drought-prone areas, with specific reference to a village. The study is based on preliminary information obtained on a visit to the village, as a prelude to a larger study on 'Drought and Sustained Development'. The second section deals with brief description of the village and the crisis faced by it. The third section tries to explore the underlying causes. The last section, is an attempt to raise larger questions regarding 'drought and sustainability of development'.

II

For a chronically drought prone Anantapur district, Atmakur, alongwith two of its hamlets Kurplapalli and Kothapalli, is an unusually large village with a population of 6843 and a geographical area of 23.23 sq. miles. With no irrigation tank, the village is entirely dependent on rainfall and well irrigation for cultivation. Over the years the village has been undergoing severe ecological stress which may be seen from the changes in population growth, workforce composition, drinking water for human beings and the livestock, landuse, cropping pattern and the use of common lands.

Table 1 presents data relating to changes in population and workforce over two decades, 1961-1981. The rate of growth of population has been lower than the national average. This is not unusual for a drought-prone area. But compared to 1.62 per cent in 1960s, the growth rate declined to 1.14 per cent in 1970s. The changing definition of 'workers' from census to census makes comparison of the workforce data, without proper adjustments, rather tenuous. A cursory look at the data does reveal that there has been slowing down of growth of workforce indicating a possibility of migration. A definite evidence can be had from the negative growth rate of 2.46 per cent of male agricultural labourers during the 1970s. Household industry which had a workforce of 435 in 1961 declined to 202 in 1971 and 174 in 1981, a contraction from 17 per cent share in the workforce in 1961 to 6 per cent in 1981. It is of interest to note here that in 1971 there was a Weavers' Co-operative Society and a Neera and Date Jaggery Co-operative Society in the village but there was none when we visited in 1990. With the decline of the household industry, the proportion of workforce in agriculture (cultivators and agricultural labourers) which remained at 70 per cent in 1961 and 1971 increased to 75 per cent in 1981—a curious structural adjustment indeed. It would be interesting to look into the wage rates, the intensity of employment etc., but as yet we have no data.

Until the late 1970s the villagers were drawing their requirements of domestic and drinking water from the open dug wells which had oil engines for irrigation. This was the source of drinking water for livestock as well. Besides, there were about 15 household wells supplying for domestic use. But by the end of 1970s most of these dug-wells and the household wells dried up. Since 1980 the sole source of water supply has been a dugwell with an inwell bore. Piped water is supplied to the village from an overhead tank through tap outlets at important corners. Since the entire village depends on this single source of water there has been enormous pressure on the supplies especially during the summer months, resulting in acute scarcity.

Atmakur and the neighbouring villages were known for sheep rearing. But in recent years lack of adequate grazing land and drinking water resulted in many sheep co-operatives financed under the DPAP becoming defunct. Scarcity of fodder and drinking water forced farmers to resort to distress selling of cattle. The residential area of Atmakur is surrounded on all sides by tamarind trees which constitute the common property of the village. But in recent years many of these trees have been drying up because of depletion of the water table to the depths beyond the reach of these trees. This is experienced ever since there has been competitive drilling of in-well bores.

III

In understanding the present ominous crisis in Atmakur we have to take a close look at the changes in the moisture regime as an important explanatory factor. These changes may best be analysed by considering them in their components of rainfall, surface water use, ground water exploitation and cropping pattern.

Rainfall: Table 2 presents rainfall of the village for twenty years, 1971-90. It shows that rainfall in Atmakur has not only been low but extremely variable ranging from 225 mm to 1000 mm, with mean of about 700 mm. However, there is no secular trend, though one may notice an increase in the fluctuation for the later period of 1970-90. It would be too much of a speculation at this stage to consider these increasing variations in the later period as a consequence of deteriorating vegetative cover affecting the connective rainfall, though not that of monsoon. For the present we may proceed that there is no trend in the Atmakur rainfall. In other words the changes in Atmakur economy and ecology cannot be blamed on declining rainfall. This leaves us with the human interventions with the moisture regime in the form of storage of run-off, use of ground water and the nature of crops grown.

Surface Water: Atmakur village has no irrigation tanks but two large percolation tanks which have been converted into private lands for cultivation. One of the major causes for the present water crisis in the village appears to be the conversion of the two public percolation tanks into private property. One of these two percolation tanks is located close to the village at an elevated area supposed to hold the run off from the up-lands and the other is located at a distance of two kilometres at a lower end of the village with a catchment of some hillocks and uplands. Though the exact years are yet to be found out the information from the village suggests that until the 1950s these two percolation tanks were effective in collecting the run-off from the South-West monsoon and the storage served not only as effective percolation to maintain the water table in the dugwells but also as a source of drinking water for livestock. Though it is not exactly known how these percolation tanks, the common property of the village, became private land, one may conjecture that during the Grow More Food Campaign when tank-bed lands were assigned to cultivators for raising food crops, lands in these two tank beds might have passed into the private hands. These hands must have caused the breaches which have never been repaired. For over three decades now these percolation tanks have only huge bunds which are the public property and tank beds which are 'patta' private land! The major claimants to these tank bed lands happen to be the two dominant land owners, one in each of the two tanks. And besides the privilege of owning the tank beds, they share among themselves and their in-laws the positions of democratically elected offices of *panchayat* presidentship, co-operative bank directorships, positions for their children in civil services etc. The gravity of this process of privatisation of public property was not fully realised until the late 1970s when yet another private entreprenurial zeal set a process that now threatens the very survival of the village economy. And this is related to the groundwater exploitation for irrigation.

Ground Water Exploitation: Since there are no irrigation tanks, the only source of irrigation is wells which are dependent on private investment. With the given rainfall, and deliberate encroachment upon the percolation tanks in favour of private gain of a few individuals, the crux of the scarcity of water in the village depends entirely on the behaviour of the exploitation of groundwater by wells. Detailed data on the number of wells, season-wise area irrigated and extent of energisation are available for the period 1971-72—1987-90. Information from the village suggest that there were as many as 170 dugwells with at least one-third of them fixed with diesel engines before 1971. But by 1971-72 the number of wells declined to 141 and the diesel engines to about 35. Table 2 presents data relating to the rainfall, number of wells, and season-wise area irrigated during these two phases for 1971-1990 period. The period falls into two clear phases: the first phase which may be called as the 'declining phase' spanning 1971-72 to 1979-80 and the second phase which may be termed as revival phase of 1980-81 to 1989-90. By the beginning of the first phase we could clearly see the decline had already set in and the number of wells as well as area irrigated both in Kharif and Rabi seasons show a clear declining trend, reaching the lowest level by 1979-80. It was during this period that there was increasing realisation of the depleting impact of the breached and privatised percolation tank on the water table. The abandoning of the surface storage in the percolation tank combined with the lifting of water from the wells with diesel engines precipitated a crisis which resulted in drying up of dug wells and the decline in their number of 120 and dismantling of as many as 35 diesel engines. This phase also witnessed serious drinking water problems both for human and livestock population.

1980-81 marks the beginning of the revival phase. The revival in the number of irrigation wells and the area irrigated during the Kharif and Rabi seasons was ushered by the extension of electric power for water lifting and the introduction of in-well-bore technology. By 1989-90 the number of wells increased to 130. All but one well, were equiped with an in-well bore and electric pumps. There were liberal institutional credit and in certain cases subsidies to the well owners for executing in-well-bores. This competitive spirit was further aided by the state policy of fixing the power tariff for agriculture in terms of flat rate per horse power regardless of the energy consumed! The gross area irrigated has been increasing gradually and so are the disasterous consequences. The water table is depleting so fast that a few in-well-bores have dried up. At least three wells have already been fixed with two motors each to lift water in two stages. Some of the tamarind trees in the village commons have started drying up in the recent years.

A close analysis of the information in table 2 reveals certain interesting aspects of the irrigation achieved at a heavy investment to the private well owners and a grave ecological threat to the very sustenance of human, animal and plant life of the village. It is observed that during the entire period, the area irrigated was higher during the Kharif compared to the Rabi. The latter never exceeded one-third of the gross irrigated areas. A word of explanation is necessary here. Atmakur lies in the rain-shadow area and receives even the meagre rainfall only during the South-West monsoon which falls in the Kharif season. The entire region is therefore a single season, *i.e.*, Kharif crop area. The irrigated area under Kharif has been more because it is largely supplementing the monsoon. In spite of this fact the area irrigated to the net sown area during the Kharif has been in the range of only 4 to 7 per cent (Table 3). In other words the grave dangers to which the village economy and ecology are subjected to are in return for the benefit of a small fraction of the total area cultivated. Further the village has about 1200 households and only 129 wells with bores drilled and energised are the sources of the problem. Given the fact that there are a few households with two or three wells, about 10 per cent of the households irrigating about five per cent of the net sown area and among themselves only a few occupying the percolation tanks, have been responsible for pushing the entire village to the brink of the sustainability. Further, the area irrigated per well which declined in the first phase, has started increasing in the second phase. One of the contributing factors to this increase may be the power tariff policy which has all the incentives for overuse of the installed power capacity. This phenomenon also may have induced the well owners to prefer water-intensive crops. However, average irrigated area under a well still remains at a low level of four acres even in the best of the seasons like Kharif of 1989-90. The limits to the exploitation may be seen from the Rabi irrigation which never exceeded an average of 1.55 acres per well, with the exception of 1987-88 which appears to be an unusual year in many respects.

Cropping Pattern: Cropping pattern is another important aspect of the moisture regime which has often been looked upon as a possible source of effecting some conservation. Table 4 shows that during the first phase there was not only decline in the number of wells and area irrigated under wells but also a very steep contraction in the area cultivated. This is rather surprising in the light of the fact that irrigation accounts only for a small fraction of the net sown area and rainfall, though fluctuated, did not show any declining trend during the period. The cropping pattern also experienced rapid changes. Jowar declining from its place of primacy accounting for over 70 per cent of the Kharif crop in 1971-72 to about 28 per cent in 1979-80 and groundnut expanding from about 11 to 58 per cent during the same period.

A close look at the irrigated area and the cropping pattern (Table 4) shows that during the first phase the decline in the area under Paddy and Ragi, the traditionally irrigated crops, had been much steeper than the decline in the irrigated area itself. This reveals that during the later years of the first phase there was an effort to switch to the favour of irrigation for dry crops like groundnut by reducing Paddy and Ragi cultivation. But the reverse of it is happening during the second phase. This may be due to the energised in-well bores. In other words there has been a tendency towards re-switch to water-intensive crop like Paddy in the second phase. What is not so clear about the second phase is the increase in the overall cultivated area by more than three times? It may be necessary to look for more information before hazarding any guess on this count.

IV

Atmakur is thus a clear and conspicuous case of gross neglect of surface water and over-exploitation of groundwater, causing severe and potent irreversible ecological degradation of resources and deprivation of livelihood activities to the people. It is a clear evidence of man-made hazard in the absence of protecting institutional system. One wishes that Atmakur is an exception and the experience of other drought-prone areas are different. But the evidence is to the contrary. The question therefore is how to make development sustainable[2] in the sense of not only providing for the basic needs of the present and future generations of people in these areas but also for improvement of their quality of life. With increasing proportion of population depending on agriculture which is characterised by low and very widely fluctuating rainfall of 225 mm to 100 mm, with per capita cultivated dry land varying from half to one and a half acres between the good and the bad monsoons, with no prospect of the area irrigated exceeding not more than ten per cent of the cultivated area, with the ground and drinking water at the brink of exhaustion (*i.e.*, water itself acquiring the characteristics of an exhaustible resource), with pastures and forests disappearing into the records merely as data, with the dwindling household industry,—if the solution is not one of deserting the area,—how to sustain life in the areas like Atmakur and what kind of an approach would help in understanding and arriving at the right strategy? Could it be looked upon merely as an "economic problem which must be understood in economic terms" which would mean that the crisis of water use is a consequence of market failure which could be understood in terms of the shadow price of the scarce water resource?[3] Would the resulting policy of a 'right price' for the water use provide a solution? Or, would one approach it in game-theoretic terms which suggest that the outcome "is caused by the operation of 'the isolation paradox' whereby a socially irrational outcome is caused by the sum of unco-ordinated individual actions, none of which may be irrational within the narrowness of the individual frame of reference"?[4] Can the 'tragedy of commons'—here the surface and groundwater be solved by the Olsonian solution of 'collective action'?[5] Or can one think in terms of a technological solution of diverting water from other basins? Given the existing institutional set up, would it result in sustainable development? Or, is *in-situ* water conservation a reality? Or, would it not be possible to see more productive use of the very existing resources if there is change in the relationship between the producers if there is change in the relationship between the producers and resources? Are there any surpluses generated in these villages? For instance, what is happening to the 'surpluses' of the hundred and odd well-owning households of Atmakur? Do these surplus flow out of the village? In what form and with what kind of linkages? Can one seek answers in these 'external' linkages?

Does the answer be in dissolving or modifying these linkages? Does a suitably modified version of 'delinking approach'[6] help?

TABLE 1
Area, Population and Workforce in Atmakur

			1961	1971	1981
1.	Area (in Sq. miles)		23.23	23.23	23.23
2.	Occupied Residential Houses		961	1029	1212
3.	Number of Households		968	1062	1212
4.	Population	Persons	5200	6108	6842
		Male	2669	3112	3447
		Female	2531	2996	3395
5.	Scheduled Caste	Male	299	372	415
		Female	256	359	424
6.	Scheduled Tribe	Male	123	179	209
		Female	144	140	188
7.	Workers	Total	2542	2566	2923
		Male	1537	1744	1959
		Female	1005	822	964
8.	Cultivators	Total	998	703	1272
		Male	652	591	935
		Female	346	112	338
9.	Agricultural Labourers	Total	754	1086	921
		Male	289	509	397
		Female	465	577	524
10.	Manufacturing (Household)	Total	435	202	174
		Male	216	149	136
		Female	119	53	38
11.	Non-Workers	Total	2663	3542	3720
		Male	1137	1368	1486
		Female	1526	2174	2234

Source: District Census Handbooks of Anantapur District—1961, 1971, 1981.

TABLE 2

Area Irrigated Under Wells in Atmakur Village (in areas)

Year	Rainfall (in inches)	No. of wells	Area irrigated under wells (Acres)		
			Kharif	Rabi	Total
1971-72	20.46	141	365 (2.59)	208 (1.48)	573 (4.05)
1972-73	25.29	133	344 (2.58)	195 (2.59)	539 (4.05)
1973-74	26.64	129	308 (2.39)	186 (1.44)	494 (3.83)
1974-75	31.31	123	295 (2.40)	121 (0.98)	416 (3.38)
1975-76	9.00	120	204 (1.70)	83 (0.70)	287 (2.39)
1976-77	33.35	119	256 (2.15)	96 (0.81)	352 (2.96)
1977-78	21.91	118	278 (2.35)	83 (0.71)	361 (3.05)
1978-79	22.38	118	216 (1.82)	102 (0.86)	318 (2.69)
1979-80	9.76	120	173 (1.44)	67 (0.56)	240 (2.00)
1980-81	33.49	124	257 (2.07)	175 (1.41)	432 (3.48)
1981-82	21.84	126	292 (2.32)	147 (1.17)	439 (3.48)
1982-83	23.29	126	345 (2.73)	168 (1.33)	513 (4.07)
1983-84	15.55	127	391 (3.08)	155 (1.22)	546 (4.30)
1984-85	10.46	128	435 (3.40)	168 (1.31)	603 (4.71)
1985-86	15.20	129	486 (3.76)	192 (1.49)	678 (5.26)
1986-87	18.71	130	512 (3.94)	202 (1.55)	714 (5.49)
1987-88	20.22	130	538 (4.14)	318 (2.45)	856 (6.58)
1988-89	17.34	133	518 (3.89)	291 (2.19)	809 (6.82)
1989-90	16.92	133	507 (3.82)	274 (2.06)	781 (5.87)

Note: Figures in the brackets indicate average area irrigated under each well.

Sources: (1) Village Adangal, Atmakur Village, Fasli, 1382 to 1401 (1971-1990).

(2) Census of Minor Irrigation, Mandal Abstract, Atmakur Mandal, 1988-89.

TABLE 3
Area Cultivated and Irrigated in Kharif Season

(in acres)

Year	Area under cultivation	Area under irrigation	Percentage of irrigation to cultivation
1971-72	8,774	365	4.16
1972-73	7,816	344	4.40
1973-74	7,568	308	4.07
1974-75	6,429	295	4.56
1975-76	3,159	204	6.46
1976-77	3,581	256	7.10
1977-78	3,848	278	7.20
1978-79	3,480	216	6.19
1979-80	2,948	173	5.87
1980-81	3,749	257	6.86
1981-82	4,829	292	6.05
1982-83	5,084	345	6.79
1983-84	5,796	391	6.75
1984-85	6,795	435	6.40
1985-86	8,226	486	5.90
1986-87	10,421	512	4.91
1987-88	12,652	538	4.25
1988-89	11,824	518	4.38
1989-90	11,648	507	4.35

Note: Figures are adjusted to the nearest value.

Source: Village Adangal, Atmakur village 1382 to 1401 (1971 to 1990).

TABLE 4
Cropping Pattern in Kharif Season

Year	Groundnut	Jawar	Korra	Paddy	Ragi	Others	Total
1971-72	991	6,186	983	202	228	184	8,774
1972-73	836	5,666	828	149	164	172	7,816
1973-74	1,729	4,359	931	159	106	288	7,568
1974-75	2,463	2,835	617	109	71	334	6,429
1975-76	1,419	1,131	449	44	28	88	3,159
1976-77	1,819	1,067	455	39	47	154	3,581
1977-78	1,853	1,076	638	81	58	138	3,848
1978-79	1,794	1,166	408	63	28	147	3,490
1979-80	1,719	814	248	15	12	150	2,948
1980-81	2,077	1,177	292	41	26	135	3,749
1981-82	3,008	1,323	256	63	43	135	4,829
1982-83	2,064	895	229	122	61	66	5,084
1983-84	4,243	544	346	121	33	209	5,796
1984-85	5,525	605	217	211	27	211	6,795
1985-86	6,622	1,053	156	148	58	214	8,226
1986-87	8,931	771	219	208	94	198	10,421
1987-88	10,603	1,038	64	531	152	266	12,652
1988-89	9,874	1,186	144	506	87	227	11,824
1989-90	9,927	968	87	428	125	93	11,648

Note: Figures are adjusted to the nearest acre.
Source: Same as Table 3.

REFERENCES

1. Bardhan, Pranab (1984): *The Political Economy of Development*, Delhi, OUP, p. 6.
2. The World Commission on Environment and Development (1987): *Our Common Future*, Delhi OUP, p. 43-66.
3. Jeffrey, James, "Growth, Technology and the Environment in Less Developed Countries: A Survey" *in* Streeten, P. (ed.), *Recent Issues in World Development.*
4. Hardin, G. (1973): "The Tragedy of Commons" *in* Daly, H.E. (ed.) *Towards a Steady-State Economy*, W.H. Freeman.
5. Olson, M. (1977): *Logic of Collection Action*, Harvard.
6. The global analysis of 'delinking' is set out in Samir Amin (1983), *The Future of Maoism*, MRP, Senghaas, D. (1985), *The European Experience: A Historical Critique of Development Theory*, Dover, NH, and Senghaas, D. (1988), "European Development and the Third World", *Review*, Winter.

13

Sustainable Growth for an Island Economy: A Case Study of Andaman and Nicobar Islands

Alak Ghosh

The Andaman and Nicobar Islands—an Indian Union Territory in the Bay of Bengal—with diverse geo-climatic conditions, a multiethnic demographic composition with wide variation in needs and customs, stand out as a formidable challenge to working out an all purpose strategy for achieving sustainable growth and development. The problem of sustainability of development assumes greater significance for the resource poor, small economies which derive a major portion of their income from natural resources. Andaman and Nicobar Islands constitute a typical example of such an economy. The strategy of sustainable development in their case should relate the existing resource endowment and the basic ecological and environmental features with the proposed export-led growth strategy.

We shall attempt to show that a slow-tempo activity, based on piecemeal planning will fail to deliver the goods. India's first Prime Minister—Jawaharlal Nehru believed that the development of tribal island economies like Andaman and Nicobar requires gradual tapping of indigenous resources like forest wealth and other natural attributes. The result was that during first forty years (1950-90) of planned development of the Indian mainland, Andaman and Nicobar was virtually outside the orbit of the centralised planning mechanism. In fact, Andaman and Nicobar opted for slow, step-by-step development, as a result of which a serious imbalance was created between the development tempo of mainland India and the eco-systems of Andaman and Nicobar. We believe that there is an urgent necessity of establishing a free port in Andaman and Nicobar to facilitate trade and commercial exchanges to and from the Islands to the rest of the world. We are also of the opinion that at least fifteen to twenty of the 265 islands which comprise the whole group should be selected as growth centres or focal points for initiating the process of future rapid development. Foreign investments without political ties may be attracted at these focal points. Indian investments, if necessary with NRI collaboration and government guidance, for building and extending the infrastructural facilities, should go for all-out development. Tourism, marine fishery and wood-based industries may provide the initial big push necessary to bring out the eco-systems of these islands from the present low level equilibrium trap. In short, we advocate a variant of the strategy of export-led growth for the rapid development and transformation of Andaman and Nicobar islands. But the major focus should be on achieving a process of sustainable growth.

Introduction

Despite more than four decades of intense development activities in the developing world, the divergence between the economic and social conditions of the rich and poor countries has continued to widen. Increasing pressure of population growth on the limited supply of natural resources had led to widespread desertification of land, soil erosion, deforestation and a serious depletion of the capacity of nature to sustain the lives of hundreds of millions of people in poor countries. Modern technology based development programmes by seriously undermining the capacity of nature to rejuvenate itself has also undermined the sustainability of traditional sharing societies which depend to a great extent on nature for their survival.

As the world approaches the 21st century the question being posed by development economists and other social scientists is how economic growth and development in poor countries can be sustained. The problem of sustainability of development assumes greater significance for those resource-poor, small economies which derive a major proportion of their income from the nature. Andaman and Nicobar Islands constitute a typical example of such an economy. The strategy of sustainable development in their case should relate the existing resource endowment and the basic ecological and environmental features with the proposed policies of export-led growth. Both in the case of mainland India and the Andaman and Nicobar Islands our resource use, particularly our natural resources, should substantially improve, then growth will become more sustainable in the long run. Better use of water, better use of minerals and better use of land and forests will bring about an improvement in the incremental capital-output ratio (ICOR), accelerate the growth process and will be conducive for achieving the process of sustainable development.

The purpose of this article is to examine the present socio-economic scenario of Andaman and Nicobar Islands, with a total area of 8,249 sq. km. constituting an Indian Union Territory. The Andaman and Nicobar Islands, with diverse geo-climatic conditions, a multi-ethnic demographic composition with wide variation in needs and customs, stand out as a formidable challange to working out an all-purpose strategy for achieving sustainable growth and development.

During first forty years (1950-90) of planned development of the Indian mainland, Andaman and Nicobar was virtually outside the orbit of the centralised planning mechanism as emphasised in India's Five Year Plans. In fact, Andaman and Nicobar opted for slow, step-by-step development, as a result of which a serious imbalance was created between the development tempo of mainland India and the eco-systems of Andaman and Nicobar. We believe that there is an urgent necessity of establishing a free port in Andaman and Nicobar to facilitate trade and commercial exchanges to and from the Islands to the rest of the world. We are also of the opinion that at least fifteen to twenty of the 265 islands which comprise the whole group should be selected as growth centres or focal points for initiating the process of future rapid development.

Foreign investments without political ties may be attracted at these focal points. Indian investments if necessary with NRI or non-NRI collaboration and government guidance for building and extending the infrastructural facilities, should go for all-out development. Tourism, marine fishery and wood-based industries may provide the initial big push necessary to bring out the eco-systems of Andaman and Nicobar from the low level equilibrium trap in which it was submerged for nearly fifty years even after Indian independence. In short, we advocate a variant of the strategy of export-led growth for the rapid development and transformation of Andaman and Nicobar Islands.

The Eco-Systems of Andaman and Nicobar Islands

Andaman and Nicobar Islands, which lie in the Bay of Bengal, are 1,255 km. from Calcutta and 1,190 km. from Madras. These Islands comprise a total area of 8,249 sq. km. and a total population of 1,88,741. Five islands grouped together are called the Great Andamans and to the south is the Island of Little Andaman. There are some 204 islets, with two principal groups being the Ritchie Archipelago and the Labyrinth Islands. The Nicobar Islands are situated to the south of the Andamans—121 km. from Little Andaman. Port Blair is the capital of Andaman and Nicobar Islands. The jurisdiction of Calcutta High Court extends over these Islands.

Japanese forces occupied the Andaman and Nicobar Islands in 1942. The British re-occupied them in 1945. The British Government used the islands mainly as a final settlement for life and long-term convicts. After independence the Islands became an Indian Union Territory and was put under the charge of a Lt. Governor.

The original inhabitants of Andaman and Nicobar mostly live in the forests and depend on hunting and fishing for their livelihood. Besides the tribal population, we have a population of displaced families from East Pakistan (now Bangladesh) who were settled in the Islands in 1967.

Forests cover 7,130 sq. km. of the total area of the Islands. All types of forest are found in the Islands. But good variety of timber is found mainly in the Andaman group of Islands. The water around the Islands is exceptionally rich in fish. However, unlike the Indian main-land, there is no traditional fishing community in the Islands.

There are 466 small scale and handicraft industrial units besides a few large sized industrial units. The large scale units are mainly wood-based establishments located in and around Port Blair, and Bamboo Flat in South Andaman. The products of large-sized industrial units comprise sawn timber, commercial plywood, match splints and veneers.

There are more than twenty power houses in the Islands. The Phoenix Bay power house is the main source of power to Port Blair (capital) and nearby areas. Out of the total of 390 inhabited villages, 272 were electrified till December 1989. These Islands possess unique species of flora and fauna. The scenic beauty all around the Islands is charming and attracts both Indian and foreign tourists.

Constraints to Development

First, we have to note that from the viewpoint of overall Indian national defence the Andaman and Nocobar Islands occupy a strategic position and, therefore, the Defence Ministry may not agree to permit unlimited entry of foreign investors and foreign tourists. But some areas in the bigger islands may be chosen as focal points of development or growth centres and here foreigners may be allowed to come as tourists or investors.

Secondly, limits to growth also arise from ecological and environmental consideration. The Andaman and Nicobar Islands have an unique tropical eco-system, with wide range of diversities. The mangrove-based eco-system and the inaccessible type of the region, have allowed the unique eco-system to be preserved for a long-time in its original form. The mangroves represent important specialised plant systems supporting a diversity of animal species and rich alluvial deposits. To keep the natural eco-system in these Islands intact, as far as possible, developmental activities connected with cultivation should first be taken up in barren lands and then extended to areas arising out of cutting old and matured trees. It should be remembered that 86 per cent of the total area of Andaman and Nocobar Islands is under forest cover.

Because of the fragility of the eco-system of the Islands, the area under forest should not be seriously depleted. That is why, we are advocating a selective development of certain areas with high growth potential rather than haphazard development embracing most of the Islands. In fact, a delicate balance has to be struck between the objectives of economic growth and the imperatives of ecological restraint. There should be an overall plan to avoid large-scale environmental damage to the Islands.

Thirdly, there is an extremely poor transport network with equally poor communication back-ups between the mainland and Islands. Since well developed transport and communication facilities are the most fundamental preconditions for economic development, the shipping and air link between the mainland India and the Islands should immediately be strengthened with proper back-ups. Perhaps, a Master Plan for transport development should precede the Master Plan for the development of tourism, fishery and agro-industries.

Fourthly, Andaman and Nicobar Islands also lack other infra-structural facilities like power, harbours and jetties, staff quarters, hospitals, schools and colleges. Electricity, water supply and telecommunication facilities are most inadequate. The Government of India should take an active interest in the development of Andaman and Nicobar Islands and immediately announce a Master Plan for allround development of these Islands.

Lastly, we come to the demographical constraint. The growth up-to-date of population in the Andamans is mainly due to artificial causes connected with immigration and not so much because of natural causes. The Islands are sparsely populated without much semiskilled and skilled labour force.

Therefore, our developmentalist approach for piercing the vicious circle of poverty in the Islands should take cognizance of the demographic, ecological and strategic limits inherent in the resources and the location of the Islands chain. Nevertheless, turning to the export-led developmental strategy, we find that the growth of large scale, export-oriented sectors like tourism, marine fishery and wood-based and agro-based industiy could trigger off potential multiplier effects in various other ancillary sectors and thereby open the possibilities of major industrial development.

Tourism Development as an Engine of Growth

Andaman and Nicobar Islands have tremendous potential and possibility for the development of tourism. These Islands are considered as a tourist paradise. Though the development of tourism in the Islands has been slow in the past but in recent years the flow of tourist traffic, both foreign and domestic, have gradually increased. The entry of foreign tourists is somewhat restricted and they are allowed to visit only five Islands in the Andamans. The Indian tourists also require a permit to visit Car Nicobar and certain other islands. These Islands abound in finest type of tropical forest, underwater coral life, sandy beaches and meandering creaks. The geographical proximity to the countries of South-East Asia, from where, and to which, major international maritime routes either commence or terminate give these Islands an additional advantage irrespective of development of tourism and trade. In the selected tourist spots the government should set up hotels, arrange for helicopter service connecting the twenty islands specially selected as tourist centres. If necessary, private investors may be asked to start good luxury hotels.

Maldives' development strategy based on marine fisheries and tourism has achieved considerable success. Government of India should not therefore miss the opportunity of developing Andaman as a tourist centre. Recently, the National Council of Applied Economic Research conducted a survey of Andaman Islands and suggested that the island known as Little Andaman may be considered for development as an International Tourist Centre. Incidentally, it should be mentioned here that Little Andaman is in the middle of the shipping route from South East Asia to India. If Little Andaman is opened for foreign tourist traffic, it will definitely attract tourists because of its scenic beauty. Moreover, if Little Andaman becomes the main tourist centre, then the system of granting permits to foreign tourists should be liberalised and other restrictions should either be withdrawn or modified

Except in Port Blair, where a few three star and one five star hotel have been set up, there are almost no facilities of accommodation, transport and communication available for tourists in other islands. It is interesting to note here that recently the Association of Indian Engineering Industry (AIEI) has proposed a Free Port Project for the Andamans. AIEI has shown that with an outlay of ₹300 crores during the five year period (1985-90), it is possible to target a turnover of ₹5,000 crores from the Andamans by 1990 and ₹20,000 crores by 2,000 AD. For this purpose, the Free Port Project and the boosting of tourism serve as kingpins.

We are of the opinion that a restrictive geographical area like Little Andaman can be selected as free port area into which goods and services can be imported and remain there for an unlimited period of time without levy of customs and import duties and without quota restrictions. If the Government of India cannot spare adequate funds for the implementation of the Free Port Project, selected private companies can be identified and invited to set up the requisite facilities in terms of infrastructure at their own cost. These private companies are to be given the franchise for a specified period of 25 to 30 years to operate certain services like telecommunications, helicopter service, port facilities, etc. In short, for the development of a free port and the boosting of tourism in the Andamans, a completely new infrastructure will be required and the best alternative is to attract foreign investment through a scheme of franchising for the development of power, transport, road, port etc.

Development of Marine Fishery

It is to be noted that, though, at present, the relative position of the Andaman Islands with regard to landings of fish is not encouraging, the growth rate is the highest when compared to various fishing centres of India. It is heartening to note that even without a master plan for the development of marine fishery, marine fish productions in the Islands increased at an annual compound growth rate of 5.2 per cent during the twenty year period of 1966 to 1986.

It is interesting to note here that fishing has been a traditional occupation of many of the immigrants from India to Maldives. According to the 1985 census, marine fishing in Maldives was the single largest employer of labour. Maldives' economy has prospered because of a planned programme of marine fishing development on modern lines. Subsequently, of course, tourism development has given an additional boost to Maldives' economy. The refugees from Bangladesh, who have been settled in the Andamans by the Government of India, are well-acquainted with fishing operations and can be easily inducted into marine fishing after suitable training. Most of these refugees are quite familiar with river fishing; therefore, they should naturally acquire the special skills necessary for marine fishing. Most of the fishing activity is concentrated in Andaman Islands. There is comparatively little fishing activity at Little Andaman and Great Nicobar Islands. The Islands have a total fishermen population of 2300—majority of whom are emigrants from the Indian mainland including the Bangladesh refugees.

The Government of India should draw up a crash programme for marine fishery development and for the setting up of fish processing and canning industry of the Kerala type. The marine fishery development plan should take account of infrastructure, technology and human resources together with catching, processing, marketing, servicing and material supply to enable better exploitation of the Islands' fishery resources.

In Port Blair, basic amenities of life and facilities for communication are available. Therefore, in and around Port Blair, it is possible to attract private fishing companies to operate fishing boats and set up establishments for production, processing, storage and marketing of fish and fish products. But the government should take the initiative for providing proper training facilities for the fishermen and make arrangements for water supply, electricity and boat building. It is somewhat encouraging to note that India's Seventh Five Year Plan (1985-90) envisaged a plan for setting up a modern ice plant of ten tonnes' capacity and frozen storage compartment of 25 tonnes' capacity at Port Blair. The Seventh Plan also included the programme of establishing a Fisheries Development Corporation for Andaman and Nicobar Islands in order to guide and direct the work for the exploitation of the fisheries wealth of the Islands.

If marine fisheries' development is to be undertaken on modern lines and if this is to be included under a programme of export-led growth for the Islands, then piecemeal planning with half-hearted attempts by the government, because of lack of funds, will fail to deliver the goods. A crash programme for the development of marine fishery requires bold, risk-taking private entrepreneurs who go all-out for undertaking marine fisheries' development on modern lines. The government should provide infrastructural facilities and should not grudge to give adequate concessions and suitable incentives to the new entrepreneurs and also to the co-operatives of fishermen.

The Prospects of Agro-Based Industries

Industrialisation in Andaman and Nicobar Islands started alongwith the development of forest products and a few saw mills were set up during the British rule. The first match-splint manufacturing unit was set up by the private sector company—WIMCO in 1929. After independence, particularly during India's Five Year Plans, the industrial development of Andamans revolved round the setting up of wood-based industries. In 1988, the total number of small scale industries was 612 employing 4,000 workers. Of these small industrial units, more than one-third were either wood-based or agro-based industries

Even after the completion of seven Five Year Plans, the main constraints of industrial development such as lack of power and water supply, shortage of equipments and skilled labour, transport and communication bottlenecks and inadequacies of capital and institutional finance still continue. Despite big allocations, particularly for infrastructural development, there was heavy shortfall in expenditure in most of the Plan periods. It appears that there is a tendency amongst the bureaucrats both in Delhi and Port Blair to treat the Islands as a colony for the betterment or/and prosperity of the mainland India. This type of thinking should be given up. The Islands have rich potentiality for self-sustained growth if a big push is effectively given for initiating a programme of industrialisation based on forest, fisheries and plantations.

Although, coconut and arecanut are the main plantations in the Andaman and Nicobar Islands, there are prospects for development of rubber, tea, coffee and cashewnut plantations. Recently, red palm oil has come out as an important crop in the Islands. Government is showing an active interest in developing and extracting red palm oil. Plantation of fruits like pineapple, papaya, lemon and orange are being greatly boosted in recent years. Processing and manufacturing units have already been set up and would grow further around these plantations and agricultural products.

If we want to initiate an export-led growth, it will not be enough to develop small industries catering mainly to internal demand. In our opinion Indian investors (both resident and non-resident Indians) should be given more concessions and incentives so that they are attracted to start new units for processing of latex and converting latex into raw rubber. Manufacture of rubber products like bicycle and scooter tyres can also be encouraged. Food processing units, including canning, have excellent prospects for development by progressive private entrepreneurs. The problem of industrial development in the Andamans is to attract private investors from mainland India. But it is well-known that Indian private investors are mainly guided by profit maximisation motive. They will not undertake big and new investments until the government succeeds in removing the infrastructural bottlenecks and agree to provide tax concessions and other incentives. Therefore, the first task is to allocate sufficient funds and create an effective administrative machinery so as to remove the infrastructural deficiencies. If, even after this, private investors from mainland India are not showing sufficient interest in starting new industrial units, the recent Indian mainland experiment of opening up of the economy with the help of deregulation, decontrol and a set of incentive-based liberalised measures will have to be repeated here for all round, quick development of the eco-systems of Andaman and Nicobar Islands. In most cases the Indian investor with a foreign collaborator may be allowed to start export-oriented manufacturing units on a selective basis in 15 to 20 islands where the growth centres are located.

The Strategy of Export-led Growth in the Andamans and Lessons for Small Island Eco-system

The eco-systems of Andaman and Nicobar Islands have been submerged in a low level equilibrium trap for a pretty long-time. Even after the Five Year Plans started producing some positive results towards industrialisation and dynamisation of agriculture in mainland India, the Plans failed to bring about the dynamic transformation of the Islands' economy. This was because of the depressants like the growth of an inward-looking population and acute infrastructural bottlenecks and lack of bold, risk-taking and innovative private entreprenuers. The stimulants in the shape of programmes and outlays under the Five Year Plans were neither effective nor enough to neutralise the effect of the depressants. It is high time for the Government of India to give up the step-motherly attitude and take up in an effective manner the export-led strategy of growth for the development of the Islands' eco-system.

Development of forestry, fishery, tourism, plantation and agriculture in the Islands will create new demands for different types of tools, implements and equipments. In addition, power, irrigation and water supply projects, shipping, transportation and hotels, warehouses and other building construction activities, together with processing and servicing units, will trigger off potential multiplier effects connected with income and employment generation. The ramifications and the development of ancillary sectors in this export-led approach will open up the possibilities of a major industrial breakthrough for these Islands.

Let us now draw the lessons which we get from the eco-systems of Andaman and Nicobar Islands *vis-a-vis* the Indian mainland. It is customary for a big mainland to neglect the development of the eco-systems of the small islands. In the Indian case the neglect resulted from the belief that the fast development of tribal island economies like Andaman and Nicobar will destroy the ecological balance and impair the ethnic characteristics of the population. The tempo of development was deliberately kept slow on the plea of strategic character of the Islands from the point of view of overall national defence. It is also supposed that the tribal population will not tolerate large scale degradations due to unfettered development. This type of attitude was responsible for not only delaying the process of development but also for making these small islands behave like colonies. If the islands of New Zealand or the West Indies could develop in spite of a tribal population, there is no reason for the Andamans refraining from adopting the export-led growth strategy for all-round sustainable development of their eco-systems.

The main lesson which can be derived from this study of the eco-systems of Andaman and Nicobar Islands is that the small islands' eco-systems, tagged to the eco-system of a big and prosperous mainland, usually suffer from neglect and apathy of the government. The way out is to convince the mainland government to undertake crash programmes for initiating a process of accelerated growth so that the tempo of development is almost the same in both the mainland and the small Islands. Perhaps a big push, with the help of an export-led approach, is necessary for this purpose.

REFERENCES

1. Leibenstein, H.: *Economic Backwardness and Economic Growth*. New York: John Wiley.
2. Basu, Kaushik.: *The Less Developed Economy: A Critique of Contemporary Theory*. Delhi: Oxford University Press.
3. Spiegelglas, S. & Welsh, C.J. (ed.): *Economic Development: Challenge and Promise*. New Jersey: Prentice Hall, Inc.
4. Bardhan, P.: *The Political Economy of Development in India*. Delhi: Oxford University Press.
5. Ghosh, Alak (1987): Changing Economic Scenario in 2001 A.D.: India and the World. *Indian Economic Journal*, Bombay.
6. ______ (1989): *Report on the Study on a Development Strategy for the Andaman and Nicobar Islands*. Centre for Studies in Economic Appraisal. Calcutta.
7. Chak, B.L. (1971): *Andaman and Nicobar Islands*. Publications Division, Govt. of India, New Delhi.
8. Govt. of India (1985): *Andaman and Nicobar Islands: Seventh Five Year Plan*. Port Blair.
9. National Council of Applied Economic Research, (1972): *Techno-Economic Survey of the Andaman and Nicobar Islands*. New Delhi.
10. Sen, Probhat Kumar: *Land and People of the Andamans: A Geographical and Socio-Economic Study with a short account of the Nicobar Islands*. Post-Graduate Book Mart, Calcutta.
11. Statistical Bureau, Andaman and Nicobar Islands: *Basic Statistics of Andaman and Nicobar Islands*. 1979-80 to 1987. Port Blair.

14

GIS and Economic Models as Information Systems for Sustainable Development

S.R. Harrison and P.C. Sharma

Sustainability of development is viewed as involving ecological and socio-economic components. Ready availability of data and a capacity to take a broad and multidisciplinary perspective, are seen as requirements for managing development for long-term sustainability. Geographical Information Systems (GIS), by their ability to store, integrate and manipulate a wide range of data, provide a powerful vehicle for generating the information needed for planning development and conservation. When combined with process models and economic evaluation, these allow the relationships between ecological and socio-economic variables over space and time to take into account. Substantial progress has been made in spatial modelling to aid planning and monitoring of sustainable development, but the potential of this integrated approach has not been exploited to anywhere near its potential.

Introduction

Development in the 21st century will face new imperatives from population growth and demand for food, housing, energy, health care and so on. New technology will create the opportunity to use resources in new and more efficient ways. While technologies such as the "green revolution" have conferred huge benefits in food security and self-sufficiency, they have also had adverse impacts in terms of greater reliance on capital and energy inputs, displacement of rural labour and reduction of genetic diversity.

In the last few decades, the world's resources have been depleted at an historically unprecedented rate. Also, resource developments have frequently failed to take sufficient account of linkages between industry, the environment and human welfare. The need for long run ecological and socio-economic sustainability will impose additional constraints on development planning. Such planning has substantial information requirements, and the purpose of this paper is to examine ways in which information needs can be met. This paper first reviews the nature of "sustainability" and its application to economic growth and development. Production and consumption activities which have failed to be sustainable are examined. The nature and role of information systems to aid development planning is examined. The application of Geographical Information Systems (GIS) and process models to the planning and monitoring of resource use for long-term sustainability in Third World countries is then examined, and prospects for improved information systems are discussed.

The Nature of "Sustainability"

The term "sustainable development" can be interpreted in a variety of ways, and has different meanings in different disciplines. A reasonably tight definition is needed, if information requirements are to be identified. Interest in sustainability is not new. Malthus was concerned about population growth, and neo-Malthusian growth theories have been concerned with resource depletion (*Tisdell, 1988*). The "energy crisis" of the 1970s focused world-wide attention on declining stocks of non-renewable resources. The "green" movement of the 1980s drew attention to depletion of biological resources and reduction of the capacity of the environment to absorb wastes of production and consumption. More recently, there has been a focus on ecological sustainability development (ESD), which "... provides a conceptual framework for integrating these economic and environmental objectives, so that the products, production processes and services can be developed that are both internationally competitive and more environmentally compatible" (*Department of the Prime Minister and Cabinet, 1990*). Our view is that a more scientific and broadly based framework needs to be adopted, which recognizes both physical and socio-economic impacts. Further, the emphasis should not be on how to preserve the environment, but rather how to use resources in ways which cause less disturbance to natural systems and human communities. Our concept of the requirements for sustainable development is presented in table 1. Not everyone would agree with this classification, but it does serve to demonstrate that sustainability is a multi-dimensional objective, which cannot be approached from the perspective of a single discipline, or using simplistic methods and models.

Resource sustainability: The resource base of any nation provides the means for future development. As indicated in table 1, this includes stocks of natural resources (land, minerals, primary energy sources, biological resources), man-made resources (capital and technological knowhow) and human resources (labour and managerial capabilities).

Environmental pollution may be viewed as a particular case of degradation of natural resources (usually air and water).

As well as the capacity to maintain production levels, "ecological sustainability" includes maintenance of species diversity and ecological processes, prevention of species extinctions and protection of habitat. Eco-systems are viewed as important for recreation, science, and human life-support systems (*e.g.* provision of food, maintenance of a genetic pool, absorption of greenhouse gases).

The issues of uncertainty and irreversability are particularly important with respect to ecological sustainability. Both suggest a cautious approach towards allowing resource depletion or environmental degradation.

Economic sustainability: Economists take the homocentric view that the welfare of mankind is of overriding importance: the ultimate aim of economic policy is to maximize human well-being. Resources and environmental goods need to be managed so as to provide an ongoing stream of services or "utility". Conservation is not a goal in its own right, but only a means of reserving resources for future human use. Economists are concerned with efficiency and equity of economic systems, and the extent to which the needs and wants of individuals are satisfied. Equity is sought between individuals at a point in time (intragenerational equity in access to resources), and between individuals over time (intragenerational equity). Sustainability can be regarded as an issue in intertemporal (including intergenerational) equity: an economic system is sustainable if it can continue to satisfy basic needs for food, clothing, housing, health care, quality of life, and so on for future generations. Intertemporal equity has been given prominence by the Bruntland Report, which argued that each generation should pass on to the next a wealth inheritance (of technological capabilities) of no less than it inherited (*WCED, 1987*).

The various types of resources have a degree of substitutability. To some extent, man-made capital may be substituted for natural capital. As stocks of some resources dwindle, it may be possible to substitute with other resources. Technical knowhow and greater productivity can substitute for a reduced physical resource base. Of course, increased population will lead to increase in aggregate demand for resources. Economic sustainability may be viewed at the level of the individual (a consumer or household), firm, industry, region and state or nation. From a management viewpoint, a regional emphasis is often desirable, since resource supplies are best defined on a regional basis, and since environmental problems often are observable, and subject to monitoring and control, at a regional level.

TABLE 1
The Scope of Sustainable Development

Resource/Objective	Class	Item
Natural resources	Non-living resources	Land
		Water supplies
		Minerals stocks
		Fossil fuel reserves
	Biological resources	Forests
		Fisheries
		Flora and fauna
	Ecological state	Existence of species
		Biological diversity
		Preservation of eco-systems, processes and habitats
		Resilience of eco-systems
	Environmental quality	Air quality
		Water quality
Man-made resources	Physical and financial capital	Physical infrastructure
		Plant and equipment
		Foreign exchange
	Technology	Research and development
Human resources	Labour, management	Education and training
Socio-economic criteria	Economic viability	Individual/household (income, food security, energy)
		Firms (resource access, profits)
		Regions (output, income, employment, services)
		National economy (government revenue, foreign debt)
	Social sustainability	Individuals (freedom, participation)
		Community cohesion
		Health care
Institutions		Maintenance of Law and Order
		Political stability
	Cultural sustainability	Religions, traditions, languages, cultural diversity

Ecological sustainability of economic systems, and sustainability of economic units or institutions, are not the same thing. Ecological sustainability is a necessary condition if households, firms and industries are to continue to function. But it is not a sufficient condition. Economic sustainability also depends on long-term profitability or viability of economic agents. Firms must have on-going access to resources if they are to continue to produce goods and services, and in this context economic sustainability is in conflict with conservation activities.

A distinction between the terms "growth" and "development" is made by economists. Both refer to the progress of an economic system over time. But whereas growth refers to increase in output of a nation or region (*e.g.*, as measured by gross domestic, stale or regional product), "development" implies more targeted growth, in particular areas. Thus development is concerned with the directions which growth takes, and in social progress, conservation and other goals of society.

Social sustainability: Nations, and population groups of which they are composed, typically have, a many and varied social goals. These include involvement and self-esteem of individuals, maintenance and cohesion of existing social groups (families, religious orders, social institutions), maintenance of social institutions, preservation of cultural heritage and diversity, provision of services and infrastructure, maintenance of law and order and political stability. Typically, it is not a simple matter to separate out economic and social sustainability. For example, job creation or losses fit under both these headings. Assessment of the social desirability of development programmes needs to take account of the views of local communities. This is an important level of decision-making, since it is the level at which social problems are faced, and solutions have to be made to work.

Non-Sustainable Development

One way of exploring the requirement of sustainable development is to examine situations where developments can be judged in retrospect to have had significant undesirable impacts on natural resources or communities. The history of such failures provides lessons for the future. In general, these will be cases where attention has not been paid during planning to all three systems: ecological, social and economic. Often ecological sustainability has been achieved by "locking up" resources. However, there are overwhelming needs for economic growth and development, to provide goods and services (including basic necessities) and to create jobs which provide livelihoods. While wealthy countries can afford to have large areas as national parks, this is not always possible where population pressures are great. Any form of economic development will use up some resources (including non-renewable resources) and create some waste products which must be absorbed by the environment. The challenge is to choose those developments which are least damaging in these regards. Some of the major cases of non-sustainability are listed in table 2. These adverse impacts occur at global, national, regional and local levels, and in the resource extraction, production, transport and household sectors. At the most basic level, food and energy security are the greatest issues of sustainability.

Analytical Frameworks for Sustainable Development

Information systems are only useful in as much as the information is relevant to effective resource management (planning, monitoring and control). In order to plan development strategies which are sustainable in the long run, it is necessary to devise a framework for analysis which is sufficiently broad to take account of environmental and socio-economic factors. Such a framework needs to recognize the various goals of a society, the production and development activities which may be conducted, and the resource, husbandry and other constraints which apply. Some form of multi-objective programming (*Romero and Rehman, 1989*), whether formally or informally applied, provides a useful framework.

The ecological impacts of specific development proposals may be examined through environmental impact assessments (EIA). Detailed understanding of the long-term ecological consequences of particular harvest regimes on industries such as logging and fishing can take years to obtain, so often very limited information is available for planning. Various techniques are available for determining the economic consequences of resource developments. Cost-benefit analysis (CBA) allows the net social impact of any development or conservation program to be estimated, based on changes in economic surplus. Both market and non-market (*e.g.*, air quality) goods may be valued. The technique of interindustry input-output analysis (IOA) provides information of relevance to both economic and social sustainability. This information is compatible with national and regional accounts, and indicates the regional economic and employment impacts of specific industry developments. It is less satisfactory when determining national welfare gains, since income and output measures derived by IOA are not consistent with the economic surplus concept.

TABLE 2

Examples of Non-sustainability

Activity	Consequences
Global and national issues	
Energy	Greenhouse gas emissions
	Oil price shocks
	Nuclear security
Catastrophes	Nuclear accidents, chemical accidents
Regional production activities	
Pasture and crop production	Chemical residues in water, erosion, salinity, acidification, desertification, non-site effects (road damage, siltation of water storages)
Logging and land clearing	Loss of biological resources
	Fuelwood shortage
Paper production	Deforestation and loss of forest biota
	Chlorine pollution of waterways
Irrigation	Inundation of forests, salinity, depletion of aquifer supplies
Logging	Deforestation
Afforestation	Dispossession of forest dwellers
Fishing	Depletion of stocks
Mining	Pollution of soils and waterways
	Disfigurement of landscapes
Electricity generation	Smog, acid deposition, greenhouse gases
Secondary industry	Air and water pollution, noise
	Industrial calamities
Distribution	
Transport	Vehicle emissions, noise
Households	
Domestic consumption	Domestic waste
Urban spread	Loss of arable land

Various social impact assessment methods and checklists have been devised (*Fitzsimmons, 1975; Finsterbusch and Wolf, 1981; Branch, 1984; Carley and Bustelo, 1984*). Some progress has been made in devising integrated impact assessment methods which simultaneously examine ecological, economic and social aspects; however, typically information from various sources is combined in an informal manner (*Rossini and Porter, 1983*). There is often a lack of co-ordination with respect of assessment of environmental, economic and social impacts, each of which provides partial information on the social desirability of development. Mandatory impact assessments, complex approval mechanisms, and wide-ranging inquiries impose substantial public and private costs, and can prevent or delay potentially worthwhile projects.

Information System Frameworks

The formulation of policies to achieve sustainable development requires that much comprehensive, accurate and up-to-date information be available to decision-makers. To this end, governments and non-government organizations are developing comprehensive data bases. As yet, development of environmental databases is in its infancy. Ideally, an information system will be available for examining resource, economic and social sustainability simultaneously, on a regional basis. This will provide data needed by various levels of governments (national, state and regional). Greater consistency of decisions will result if different authorities are using the same database. It is our contention that Geographic Information Systems (GIS) provide the integrating methodology for such an approach.

The nature of GIS: A GIS contains spatially and thematically referenced data usually in a relational database, and interrogation and mapping facilities (*Broscoe and Fowler, 1989*). The GIS is designed for ease of data entry and updating, and efficient storage with minimal data redundancy. GIS offer a considerable advance on the manual means typically used for data inventory, including more complex queries and more rapid response. Data from various sources may be integrated in the database. Data typically consist of a number of layers, relating to land characteristics (including soil type, vegetation, land use, topography, climate and tenure), and sometimes also infrastructure, industry and demographic data (*e.g.*, front census collections, surveys such as labour force, and by-products of administrative processes). The technology of GIS is well suited for management of large spatial data sets (*e.g., Aronoff, 1989*). GIS are designed to collect, process, analyse and manage all types of spatial land-related data. A number of software packages are available for system development, including ArcInfo (the most widely adopted), MapInfo and SPANS.

The role of GIS: The development of GIS for resource management can be seen in terms of three stages or levels, *viz.* inventory, data integration and analysis, and modelling. This conceptualization reflects the view that to formulate policies for sustainable development we need to know: (*i*) What is the existing situation? (*ii*) What changes to the existing situation are taking place? (*iii*) What will the system be like in the future if the current management regime is continued? (*iv*) What will happen if alternative managements are imposed?

The simplest type of GIS is as an inventory of resources and their characteristics. This base level operation provides a description of the present state of resources, and is a logical extension of current information recording systems. The system could include records of such variables as soils, crops, roads, climatic parameters. The next level is the move away from isolated, stand-alone inventories to that of integrated databases. In such a system data of various types and from various sources which form the basis of several databases are integrated into a single system. The requirements for such integration are well-known: for textual and attribute data there is a need for some sort of common identifiers or keys; for graphic or map data a common co-ordinate reference system is required. Thus the integration of separate soils, climatic and vegetation databases allows the possibility of making inferences about rangeland potential—clearly, a piece of 'value-added information'! The highest level of GIS application is that of spatial analysis and modelling. This level itself includes possibilities ranging from relatively simple "what if' type calculations to more sophisticated process modelling.

The simpler modelling involves using GIS as a kind of "spatial spreadsheet", where the system is interrogated with "what if' questions and it responds by accessing one or more layers of information. For example when planning afforestation we could ask: What area will be available if we select only land which is of moderate high natural fertility? How will the above answer change if land below certain slope is excluded (*i.e.*, made available for some other use)? What will happen if some other constraints such as farm size, rainfall, distance from a major urban area are introduced? More sophisticated modelling is more demanding on data and as well may require interfacing GIS with models developed in other disciplines such as economics. These models explore the complex interactions among variables and examine the behaviour of the system over both space and time.

These levels are build upon each other. Advanced uses should not be contemplated until attention is paid to establishment of the database. A resource inventory is a starting point for computerizing an information system. When designing this inventory system, high level uses need to be kept in mind. Once the database has been developed to a satisfactory stage, the system may be used to generate information which will assist in making decisions about resource availability under given sustainability constraints. Finally, modelling allows system behaviour over space and time for alternative management policies to be examined. The GIS allows small-area predictions from process models to be aggregated, *e.g.*, from the field to farm level, or the farm to catchment level. Viewing the application of GIS at these three levels is both conceptually defensible as well as oriented towards a financially realistic implementation programme. The allied technology of remote sensing has a proven record in the collection of resource data (especially over large area) at relatively low cost. It appears well suited for Third World countries in which little resource data is currently available, especially for "first pass systems", to be later augmented by ground truthing.

Interfacing GIS with process models: Exploring sustainability aspects of complex natural and man-made systems and their relationship with society may require modelling of biological and socio-economic processes. This allows complex interrelationships between variables over time to be taken into account, and resource levels, environmental quality, income flows and social states under alternative management scenarios to be predicted. While GIS are ideal for data management, they are not so well suited for process modelling. Although GIS software have some process modelling capabilities, often it is more efficient to interface simulation and other models with the database. The method of interfacing will depend on the complexity of analysis required. For simple types of analysis, the programming facility within GIS software may be adequate. Alternatively, it may be a simple task to carry out say discounted cash flow analysis using a spreadsheet package. More complex analysis require sophisticated programming in languages such as FORTRAN or C, and interfacing with the GIS software (*Sharma and Harrison, 1991*).

Issues to be considered in GIS design and construction: A number of issues need to be considered when setting up a GIS for resource management.

Identification of goals: Sustainability goals differ between countries, *e.g.*, food and fuelwood self-sufficiency may be a target for one country, while raising revenue through tourism may be more important to another. The effectiveness of planning and monitoring can only be assessed in terms of these goals, which are often difficult to elucidate.

Nature of information needed for planning: A GIS is by nature a repository for data with efficient means of data maintenance and access. Its use in planning adds another dimension, since the behaviour of natural and man-made systems over time in response to managements has to be predicted. A database in itself is of little predictive value unless associated with a variety of modelling and interpretation. It will be some time before GIS are used widely for regional and urban planning.

Volume of data: It is unlikely that all the data needed for planning even a relatively confined project could be included in a single database. Certainly, for a nation, the total volume of resource information "is too great for it to be held in a single centralised database—it would simply cost too much to keep a centralised database up-to-date across the whole spectrum of resource information" (*Griffiths, 1991, p. 6*).

Resource demands of database construction: Setting up a comprehensive database for planning purposes could cost tens of thousands, and perhaps hundreds of thousands, of dollars. The gathering of data on the wide range of variables is a time-consuming and expensive task. Computer hardware and software are likely to account for only a small fraction (may be 20 per cent) of the cost of setting up a comprehensive GIS for planning purposes. The time required is unlikely to be less than one year, and may be several years. For any particular planning study, there is likely to be an imperative to bring together as much as possible relevant information as quickly and at as little cost as possible. Unless planned and budgeted for in advance, it is unlikely that an effective information system will be implemented.

Resource demands for system and maintenance: It is necessary to keep a GIS up-to-date, and this can involve salaried staff and on-going data collection.

Maintaining institutional support: There have been many cases of unrealistic expectations and abandonment of costly GIS projects. Often the funding agency fails to realize the resource or time requirements. Relative to manual systems, GIS should not be expected to reduce cost initially, or to produce information more quickly. However, once established GIS should be capable of carrying out equivalent analyses at a fraction of the cost, and allowing tasks to be performed which would be impossibly time-consuming, with a manual system.

Lack of technical information: Substantial technical and other information are needed to determine the extent of adverse ecological and socio-economic impacts associated with development. Often this scientific information simply is not available.[1]

Data Sources and Collection/Capture Methods

Given our broad definition of sustainability, a wide variety of data is needed on biological, economic and social systems, their interrelationships, and their changes in response to management policies. Data will be available from a variety of agents (levels of government, private firms), between which communication and co-operation may be less than desired. Different countries are at various stages in compilation of physical resource inventories. Some of the typical sources of data are as follows:

The natural system: surveying, telemetry, field observation, maps and remote sensing;[2] established land information systems; biological resource inventories: plants, native animals, fish, registers of rare and threatened species; critical numbers to maintain populations; research and experience on carrying capacities for domestic animals, wildlife and humans (tourists); experimentation and modelling research; non-biological resource inventory: estimated reserves, rate of extraction, amount conserved and amount available to industry, climate records.

The economic system: demographic statistics (population distribution by area, age, sex, ethnicity); labour force statistics (employment, incomes), often survey-based; education and training; firms: output, profitability, resource needs; industries: numbers and sizes of firms, profitability, reliance on resource supplies; market price data, and willingncss-to-pay estimates for non-market goods; economic analysis (input-output and cost-benefit analyses).

The social/cultural system: routine official collections, *e.g.* from social security and justice departments; social surveys (on social attitudes, willingness-to-pay); community attitudes, obtained through local meetings, submissions from community groups.

Integrated ecological and socio-economic data: impact studies (environmental, economic and social); research teams (government, university); public inquiries (hearings, written submissions, rebuttals, consultancies).

Uses of Spatial Resource Information Systems

Spatial and temporal sustainability information systems have a wide range of potential uses in resource-use planning and monitoring, some of which are now outlined.

Identifying problem areas: The information handling capabilities of GIS make them useful for identifying problems with regard to resource degradation, pollution, disadvantaged groups, and so on, and to assess the seriousness of such problems. There may be a suspicion of a problem, or visual evidence, but the nature, extent and cost of that problem may be difficult to determine. A variety of scientific and socio-economic data can be stored (*e.g.* on land and vegetation, mineral deposits, population, infrastructure, environmental quality), which can be used to detect patterns of pressure on resource use and resource degradation. As well, process models can be used to predict changes in resource supplies and environmental quality. The impact of overgrazing, deforestation, overfishing, and so on may be examined.

Selection of development projects: By carrying out selections of variables from spatial databases, it is possible to examine ecological and socio-economic impacts of development proposals, *e.g.*, in mining, energy production, forestry, tourism. With a GIS, it would be possible to identify areas of forest where the topography, uniqueness of species or ecosystems, wind exposure, proximity to special landscape features (*e.g.*, lakes), archaeological significance and so make logging undesirable. Similarly, it is possible to identify areas where mining would be ecologically harmful and sites where water storage would result in unacceptable loss of ecological systems or habitat of rare or threatened species. By a process of elimination, areas in which development can safely take place can be identified.

Choosing between development and conservation scenarios: Interfacing biological process and socio-economic models with GIS allows evaluation of alternative development scenarios to be compared. In this way, it is possible to identify the nature, extent and timing of development projects which will have the least undesirable ecological and social impacts.

Critical evaluation of proposed developments: Development proposals are often thrown up by the political process, as opportunities to create employment, provide finance for regional infrastructure, create an opportunity for "value-adding" activities, diversify the economic base, earn or save foreign exchange, and so on. Projects may include afforestation (for timber and wood pulp), construction of dams and irrigation systems, mining ventures, power stations, petrochemical plants, and so on. An information system is needed to integrate the facts relevant for such an evaluation.

Carrying out mandatory impact studies: It is often a requirement of state or local government that impact studies (environmental, economic, social) be conducted along prescribed guidelines. A GIS can be a convenient integrating framework for these impact studies.

Monitoring development: To date there has been an emphasis on impact assessment at the planning stage of development projects, but little ongoing monitoring. Provided a GIS is maintained with up-to-date information, it is an effective means of monitoring the impacts of development.

Evaluation of new technology: Technology which is newly developed, or to be transferred from other locations, may be tested with simulation experiments prior to introduction. An example is the testing of cropping systems which have been modelled under the International Benchmark Sites Network for Agrotechnology Transfer (IBSNAT) project. Suitability of these agrotechnology packages for Third World countries can be screened using simulation experiments (*Harrison, Thornton and Dent, 1990*). It is proposed to interface the DSSAT system with a GIS to examine spatial aspects of technology adoption (*Thornton and Dent, 1990: Singh, Brink and Christianson, 1991*).

Specific Application Areas of Resource Management GIS

A wide variety of applications of information systems have been devised which have a primary focus on issues of resource depletion, environmental quality and economic and social sustainability. Some of the potential application areas are listed in table 3, and brief descriptions of applications in some of these areas are provided to demonstrate the versatility of the methodology.

TABLE 3

Potential Applications of Sustainability Information Systems

Global resource monitoring
Land management
Pasture management
Land reform
Agricultural marketing
Coastal management
Irrigation
Catchment management
River and lake management, hydrological modelling, flood control

Forest management
Fishing
Management of wilderness areas, parks and reserves
Monitoring of rare and threatened species of plants and animals
Prospecting and mining
Energy generation and conservation
Chemical residue monitoring
Natural hazard modelling
Regional planning
Urban encroachment on agricultural land.

Global resource monitoring: Kunderi (*1991*) describes efforts undertaken to collate two most important climate parameters—temperature and precipitation—on a global basis.

Land management: Land information systems (LIS) are one of the earliest and most important applications of information systems technology (*e.g., Burrough, 1986*). A number of applications have been made to land degradation (*e.g., Spanner et. al., 1982; Legis, 1983; Vold et. al., 1985; Chrisman, 1986; Ventura, et. al. 1988 and Balszczynski, 1990*). GIS provide a powerful framework for assembling existing information about soil types, topography, agricultural enterprises and land degradation which has taken place, as well as farmers' practices and attitudes to land care. These data can be compiled for a target area, such as a farm, stream catchment, or local government area (LGA).

In general, agricultural GIS typically have had only rudimentary economic analysis capabilities, while farming systems models have not handled spatial aspects well. Although it is possible to compute soil losses within a GIS, it is not efficient to perform specialist analyses within a general purpose package: rather, it is preferable to develop simulation software to interface with GIS (*Burrough, 1986, p. 96*). An integrated model of the type envisaged here, known as Co-operator Tracking System (CTS), has been used in Dane County (Wisconsin, USA) since 1987, as an aid for certifying compliance with state and federal erosion control mandates (*University of Wisconsin, 1989*). Liu and Craul (*1991*) attempt to develop agricultural soil capability ratings based upon those soil characteristics that influence productivity, and those economic and geographic site parameters that influence operational economics.

Pasture management: Coughenour (*1990*) has combined geographic information systems, remote sensing and ecosystem modelling to understand and manage spatially extensive pastoral ecosystems in

North Kenya. Regional spatial data for soils, landforms, topography and vegetation have been used to compute annual ecosystem energy flows. A dynamic GIS approach is used to estimate changing distributions of plant water demand in relation to water availability. A spatial simulation model has been developed to examine regional resource exploitation patterns by pastoralists and their livestock.

Agricultural marketing: Astroth, Sandhu and Singh (*1991*) examine the usefulness of spatial allocation model building within a GIS environment, in connection with agricultural marketing in Punjab, India.

River and lake management, hydrological modelling, flood control: GIS have been developed to simulate water levels and boundaries for various flood sizes and to map inundated land (*e.g., McColm and Syrne, 1990*). These are useful for urban planning (*e.g.* where to allow housing) and hazard prediction. Much of the world's fertile land is close to sea level, such as river deltas, and spatial modelling allows the locations and depths of water rises to be predicted, and the effectiveness of mitigation measures to be tested. Another use of spatial hydrological models is to predict changes in marine habitat over time, *e.g.* due to rises in sea level brought about by global warming.

Hu-Lin and Huei-Shyoug (*1991*) perform solid modelling of headwater landslides in order to prescribe a better strategy for the management of a watershed Optimum management prescription for landslides can be performed to ensure that water supply in the Taipei Metropolitan District (in Taiwan) will not be jeopardised. Wu and Yih-Peng (*1991*) note that traditional inundation management is an expensive, labour intensive and time consuming process. Their objective is to implement a 3-D GIS to assess damage of an inundation and to set up guidelines for a drainage planning of a river watershed in Taiwan. Shupeng and Xiaochun (*1990*) note that floods in China have happened very often, seriously affecting construction, agriculture and industrial development. They have established four types of flood control database. The optimal flood discharge zone can be chosen, and the best transportation route for the people and properties in a submerged area can be found.

Forest management: GIS have been adopted widely in forest management (*e.g. Bowen and Pearce, 1989, Fenn and Weston, 1989*). A rainforest GIS is discussed by Stanton and Bundock (*1988*). Kearsome *et. al.* (*1991*) are concerned with the clearing of tropical rainforests which may have serious local and global consequences: they have developed a computer model at Oak Ridge National Laboratory to simulate patterns of colonisation and deforestation. Lyons and Sharma (*1991*) examine the role of a GIS in monitoring the integrated social forestry (ISF) program in the Philippines.

Wilderness areas, management of parks and reserves: Junkov (*1991*) notes that in the near future most countries will have defined forever their protected areas, and whatever habitats are not in reserves, are likely to undergo drastic reduction in terms of biological diversity and possibly, productivity. The magnitude of ecosystem conversion is practically unknown, exemplified by Costa Rica where approximations of yearly deforestation rates from 1977 to 1983 fluctuate from 25,000 to 124,000 hectares. Routine monitoring of land use changes would be an important management tool providing an ongoing base for reviewing policies and practices dealing with natural resources use. It would provide a means of detecting land use changes and facilitating public awareness of major trends; testing whether the conservation model of core protected areas, buffer zones and biological corridors is practically feasible or represents an "ectopia"; and optimising land use for production according to determined land capabilities. Campbell (*1990*) discusses the capabilities of GIS for the mapping and integration of a wide variety of spatial data required for management and planning in protected areas. Lewis (*1991*) reports an ARC/INFO GIS for game park management in Zambia.

Species monitoring: Kineman, Kineman and Keammerer (*1991*) discuss a project being implemented to construct an integrated GIS of ecological and demographic data for gorilla habitat in three contiguous African parks. Kichelmore (*1991*) notes that the greatest unknown quantity in the debate about ivory trade has been the number of elephants remaining in the central African forests. Makonbe (*1990*) uses GIS to study strategies for avoiding over-exploitation of wildlife resources of Zambia. The Queensland National Parks and Wildlife Service is establishing a management information system of rare and threatened species (*Hynes and Owens, 1991*).

Natural hazard modelling: Information systems are needed for damage prediction, damage inventory, and emergency response management systems. Models of natural hazards such as fire, flood, drought, insect plague, disease and earthquakes assist in emergency planning. The NSW Parks and Wildlife Service has a spatial model which can be used to predict the direction and speed of bushfire movement.

Regional planning: An approach for design and implementation of a computerised information system (with emphasis on natural resources) to support various decision-makers involved in district (county) level planning is described by Navalgund *et. al.* (*1991*).

Urban encroachment on agricultural land: Craven (*1991*) observes that many cities in developing countries are expanding at the expense of valuable agricultural land. Identifying and measuring the spatial extent of urban growth by traditional methods is time consuming and expensive. Remote sensing and GIS technology offer a viable alternative for data capture and analysis in a timely and efficient manner. Jampoler and Haack (*1989*) report that a major concern in the Kathmandu Valley is the urbanisation of prime agricultural land. Regional planning efforts may be enhanced by using a GIS to identify land use changes and suitability.

Future Prospects

No framework for analysis will be perfect; policy decisions based on limited information will always be required. However, the combination of GIS and process models provides a powerful means of identifying resource depletion and environmental problems, planning of management policies, and monitoring of the effectiveness of these policies over time. The potential exists to base decisions on much more comprehensive data than is normally used. Also, as communication systems and information technology improves, it is probable that national planning authorities will obtain progressively more comprehensive and more easily accessed data collections.

While the potential for GIS in devising sustainable resource management policies seems unbounded, and many systems are on the drawing boards, relatively few have been fielded to date. Those that have often been for specific administrative tasks; for example. Garner (*1990*) suggests that most land information systems are parcel based for fiscal administration and land taxation, rather than planning *per se*.

Scope exists for improvements in national data collection and management co-ordination. For example, ALIC (*1990*) identifies a need for: (*i*) identifying information needs, (*ii*) facilitating data sharing and overcoming administrative difficulties, between levels of government and public *vs.* private data sources, including incorporation of research findings, (*iii*) linking together of different databases, (*iv*) cost sharing and providing access rights, (*v*) minimal standards of data quality and presentation and (*vi*) lower scale representation of land data (not more than 1 in 100,000).

Progress in computer hardware has been rapid, with increasing processor speed, greater storage, better graphics displays and generally more reliable hardware. However, scope remains for better interfaces between software packages. More training in GIS would assist in adoption in Third World countries. In this regard, Norton-Griffiths

(*1991*) discusses the GEMS/UNITAR Africa programme, which aims to strengthen national capabilities in monitoring and assessment. The programme offers training in GIS to professional resource managers, upgrades to computer hardware and software, assistance with pilot GIS projects, and medium to long-term support in terms of networking, training and funding.

Conclusions

The concept of sustainability is coming to be recognized as encompassing more than ecological considerations, important as they may be. A range of economic and social factors also need to be considered. Data relating to a large number of environmental and socio-economic variables are needed to plan and monitor sustainable development. An efficient information infrastructure for compiling, maintaining and delivering these data is needed. GIS provide a powerful means of handling data, and can be interfaced with process models for prediction purposes. Substantial progress has been made in the development of resource databases and GIS for natural resource management. However, the scope for use of natural resource GIS is still largely unexploited.

NOTES

1. A Queensland example concerns the impacts of agro-chemicals on the Great Barrier Reef. While the potential for damage is apparent, very little is in fact known of the extent of chemical concentrations in runoff or their impact on fish breeding habitats and reef marine life.
2. Types of natural resource data and methods of capture are discussed by Bracken and Webster (*1990*).

REFERENCES

Aronoff, S. (1989): *Geographic Information Systems: A Management Perspective*, WDL Publications, Ottawa.

Astroth, J.H. and Sandhu, J.S. (1991): "Spatial Allocation Modelling within a GIS Environment: An Examination of the Movement of Agricultural Goods in a Peasant Economy", Proceedings of the Eleventh Annual ESRI User Conference, pp 505-506.

Blaszczynski, J. (1990): "Regional Soil Loss Prediction Utilizing the RUSCLE/GIS Interface", Proceedings of the ASTM International Symposium on Mapping and Geological Information Systems, San Francisco.

Bowen, P.J. and Pearce, C.J. (1989): "The Use of GIS in Forest Resource Inventory", Proceedings of the 17th Australasian Conference on Urban and Regional Planning Information Systems", Perth.

Branch, K. (1984): *Guide to social assessment: a framework for assessing social change*, Westview Press, Boulder.

Broscoe, D. and Fowler, R. (1989): "Geographic Information Systems: What are they and what do they do?", reprinted from *Northpoint*, 26(4) by Intera Renting.

Burrough, P.A (1986): *Principles of Geographical Information Systems of Land Resources*, Monographs on Soil and Resources Survey No. 12, Clarendon Press, Oxford.

Campbell, K. L. (1990): "Using GIS for Wildlife Conservation in Tanzania: possibilities and prospects", Proceedings Resource Technology 90, Washington, pp 265-274.

Carley, M.J. and Bustelo, E.S. (1984): *Social impact assessment and monitoring: a guide to the literature*, Westview Press, Boulder.

Coughenour, M.B. (1990): "A GIS/RS Modelling Approach for a Pastoral Ecosystem in Kenya", Proceedings Resource Technology 90, Washington, pp 599-608.

Craven, D. (1991): "Urban Change Detection in Kathmandu", Technical Papers, ACSM-ASPRS Annual Convention, Baltimore, pp 41-50.

Dearsome, K.C. *et. al.* (1991): "Linking Spatial Data to a Model of Colonisation and Deforestation of Rondonia, Brazil", Proceedings of the Eleventh Annual ESRI User Conference, pp 157-158.

Department of the Prime Minister and Cabinet (1990): *Economically Sustainable Development: A Commonwealth Discussion Paper*, AGPS, Canberra.

Di, X. (1991): "Environmental Planning Study for a Local Government", Proceedings of the Eleventh Annual ESRI User Conference, pp 415-419.

Fenn, G.R. and Weston, K.A. (1989): "The Impact of GIS Technology on Forest Management and Forest Managers—Five Years Experience", Proceedings of the 17th Australasian Conference on Urban and Regional Planning Information Systems", Perth.

Finsterbusch, K and Wolf, C.P. (1981): *Methodology of social impact assessment*, 2nd edn., Hutchinson Ross Pub. Co., Stroudsburg, Pa.

Fitzsimmons, S.J., Stuart, L.I., and Wolf, P.C. (1975): *Social Assessment Manual; A Guide to the Preparation of the Social Well-Being Account*, US Bureau of Reclamation, Washington DC.

Garner, B.J. (1990): "GIS and Urban and Regional Planning in Australia", Chap. 3 of *Geographic Information Systems: Developments and Applications*, Belhaven Press, London.

Griffiths, A. (1990): "Information Requirements for Sustainable Development", Address to the AURISA '90 Conference, Canberra.

Harrison, S.R., Thoruton, P.K. and Dent, J.B. (1991): "The IBSNAT Project and Agricultural Experimentation", *Agricultural Experimentation.*

Hynes, R.A. and Owens, C.D. (1991): "Managing Queensland's Nature Conservation Resources", *Urisa News*, No. 36, June, pp. 18-20.

Jampoler, S. and Haack, B. (1989): "Use of GIS to Identify Land Use Change: Kathmandu, Nepal" Technical Papers, ACSM-ASPRS Annual Convention, pp 56-64.

Junkov, M. (1991): "Application of GIS in Conservation for Development Work in Central America—ICUN/ORCA", Proceedings of the Eleventh Annual ESRI User Conference, pp 155-156.

Kineman, J., Kineman, P. and Keammerer, W. (1991): "Developing a GIS Database for Park Management in the Virunga Volcanoes National Parks of Rwanda, Uganda and Zaire", *Ibid.*, pp. 43-48.

Kunderi, K. (1991): "Climate Data in UNEP's Global Resource Information Database (GRID)", *Ibid.*, pp. 371-372.

Legis, R.P.L. (1983): "Computer Mapping Techniques for Assisting Land Evaluation and Assessment of Erosion Hazards in Kisii, Kenya", M.Sc. Thesis, Wegeningen.

Lewis, D. (1991): "A Drum Beat Away from ARC/INFO's Role in Africa's Land Use Planning", Proceedings of the Eleventh Annual ESRI User Conference, pp. 115-120.

Liu, R. and Craul, P. (1991): "A GIS Based Soil Capability Classification for Agriculture in Yuisu County, China", Technical Papers ACSM-ASPRS Annual Convention, pp. 98-106.

Lyons, K.J. and Sharma, P.C. (1989): "Spatial Information as Regional Infrastructure for Economic Development, Environmental Management and Social Planning", Paper presented to the Royal Society of Queensland Symposium on *Rural Queensland—a Sustainable Future: the Application of Geographic Information Systems to Planning and Management*, Brisbane.

—, (1989): "Some Non-Technology Aspects of GIS Implementation with Particular Reference to Less Developed Countries", University of Queensland.

Makonbe, W.M. (1990): "The Development and Implementation of Wildlife Utilisation on Sustainable Yield: the Zimbabwe experience", Proceedings Resource Technology 90, Washington, pp. 514-518.

McColm, G.A. and Syme, W.J. (1990): "Integration of Flood Modelling Process with a Geographic Information System", Proceedings of the URISA Conference, Edmonton.

Michelmore, F. *et. al.* (1991): "Elephant Population Estimates for the Central African Forests", Proceedings of the Eleventh Annual ESRI User Conference, pp 49-58.

Navalgund, R.R. *et. al.* (1991), "Natural Resources Information System for District Level Planning", *Ibid.*, pp. 419-420.

Norton-Griffiths, M. (1991): "The GEMS/UNITAR Africa program: Strengthening National Capabilities in Monitoring and Assessment for Sustainable Development and Utilisation of Natural Resources", *Ibid.*, pp. 5-14.

Romero, C. and Rehman, T. (1989): *Multiple criteria analysis for agricultural decisions*, Elsevier, Amsterdam.

Rossini, F.A. and Porter, A.L. (eds.) (1983): *Integrated Impact Assessment*, Westview Press, Boulder.

Sharma, P.C. and Harrison, S.R. (1991): "Feasibility and Application of GIS Linked with Economic Models for Natural Resource Policy in Australia", Proceedings of URISA Conference, Los Angeles.

Shupeng, C. and Xiaochun, D. (1990): "Application of ARC/INFO in the Database Development of Flood Control in China", ESRI User Conference, Redlands, California, Vol. 1, pp. 1-10

Singh, U., Brink, J.E. and Christianson, C.B. (1991): "Application of the Ceres-Sorghum Model and Geographic Information Systems in the Indian Semiarid Tropics", International Fertilizer Development Centre, Muscle Shoals, Alabama.

Spanner, M.A., Strahler, A.H. and Estes, J.E. (1982): "Soil Loss Prediction in a Geographic Information System Format", Proceedings of the 16th International Symposium on Remote Sensing of Environment, Buenos Aires.

Stanton, G. and Bundock, B. (1988): "Development of the Queensland Government Rainforest Geographical Information System", Proceedings of the 16th Australasian Conference on Urban and Regional Planning Information Systems, Sydney.

Thornton, P.K. and Dent, J.B. (1990): Using Models to Explore Farming Alternatives. *Agrotechnology Transfer*. 11, 1-9.

Tisdell, C. (1988): "Sustainable Economic Growth, Production and Development: An Overview of Concepts and Changing Views", *Indian Journal of Quantitative Economics*, 4(1): 73-86.

University of Wisconsin (1989): "Land Information Technology at Work: Modernizing Land Conservation Management Systems", *Wisconsin Land Information Newsletter*, 5(1): 1-11.

Ventura, S.J., Chrisman, N.R., Connors, K., Gurda, R.F. and Martin, R.W. (1988): "A Land Information System for Soil Erosion Control Planning", *Journal of Soil and Water Conservation*, 43(3): 230-233.

Vold, T., Sondheim, M.W. and Nagpal, N.K. (1985): "Computer Assisted Mapping of Soil Erosion Potential", *Canadian Journal of Soil Science*, 65: 411-418.

WCED (World Commission on Environment and Development) (1987): *Our Common Future,* Oxford University Press, Oxford.

Wu, M., Chen, Y. and Lin, H. (1991): "Inundation Management Using a 3-D GIS" Technical Papers, ACSM-ASPRS Annual Convention, pp. 245-249.

Wu, M., Yang, H. and Song, D. (1991). "Solid Modelling of Headwater Landslides for Management of a Watershed", *Ibid.*, pp. 250-256.

List of Contributors

1. Dr. Raj Kumar Sen
   Department of Economics,
   Rabindra Bharati University,
   Calcutta, India.

2. Dr. K.C. Roy
   Department of Economics,
   University of Queensland,
   Australia.

3. Dr. Suhas Chakraborty
   Department of Economics,
   S.A. Jaipuria College,
   Calcutta, India.

4. Dr. Veena Devasthali
   Department of Economics,
   SNDT Womens' University,
   Mumbai, India.

5. Dr. Dhirendra Nath Kumar
   Kalyani University,
   Kalyani, India.

6. Dr. D.D. Guru
   Professor,
   Economic Division,
   and
   A.N. Sinha
   Institute of Social Studies,
   Patna, India.

7. Dr. N. Manonmoney
   Department of Economics,
   Madurai Kamraj University,
   Tamilnadu, India.

8. Dr. Prakash
   Professor,
   NIEPA,
   New Delhi, India.

9. Smt. Sumitra Chowdhury
   NIEPA,
   New Delhi, India.

10. Dr. P.L. Sablok
    Professor of Economics,
    Jiwaji University,
    Gwalior, India.

11. Dr. K.P. Nath
    North Eastern Hill University,
    Mizoram Campus,
    Aizawl,
    Mizoram, India.

12. Professor Amar. S. Yumnam
    Manipur University,
    Imphal, India.

13. Dr. K. Nageswara Rao
    Head,
    Department of Economics,
    S.K. Devaraya University,
    Anantapur, India.

14. Professor Alak Ghosh
    Professor of Economics,
    University of Calcutta,
    Calcutta, India.

15. Dr. S.R. Harrison
    Department of Economics,
    University of Queensland,
    Australia.

16. Dr. P.C. Sharma
    University of Queensland,
    Australia.

Index